Adult Coloring Book:
I Need a Vacation

SALLY CANARIO & SUMMER CANARIO

ISBN: 1530055105
ISBN-13: 978-1530055104

DEDICATION

This book is dedicated to Stuart Canario, supportive husband and fantastic father. Thanks for the great memories captured in this book.

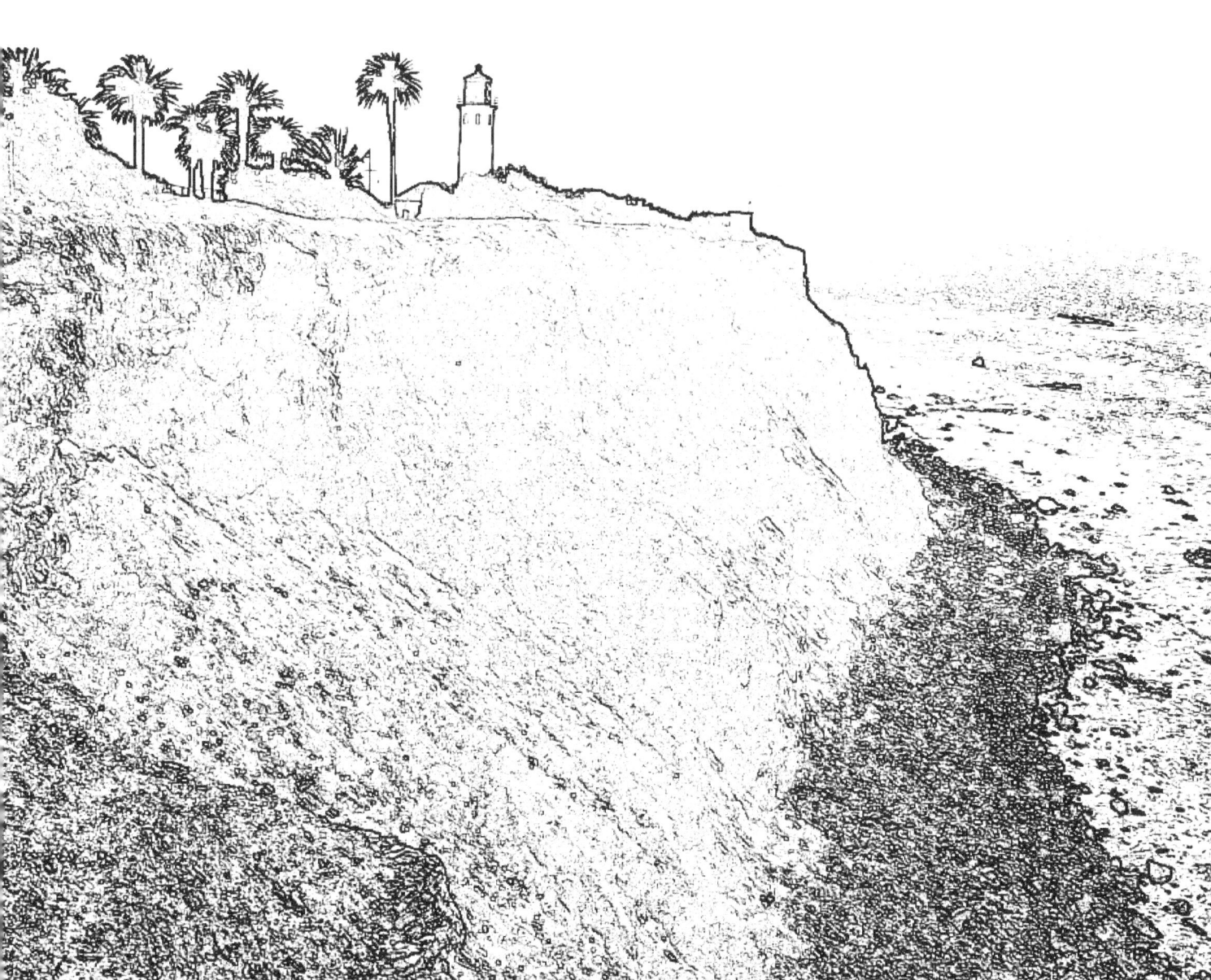

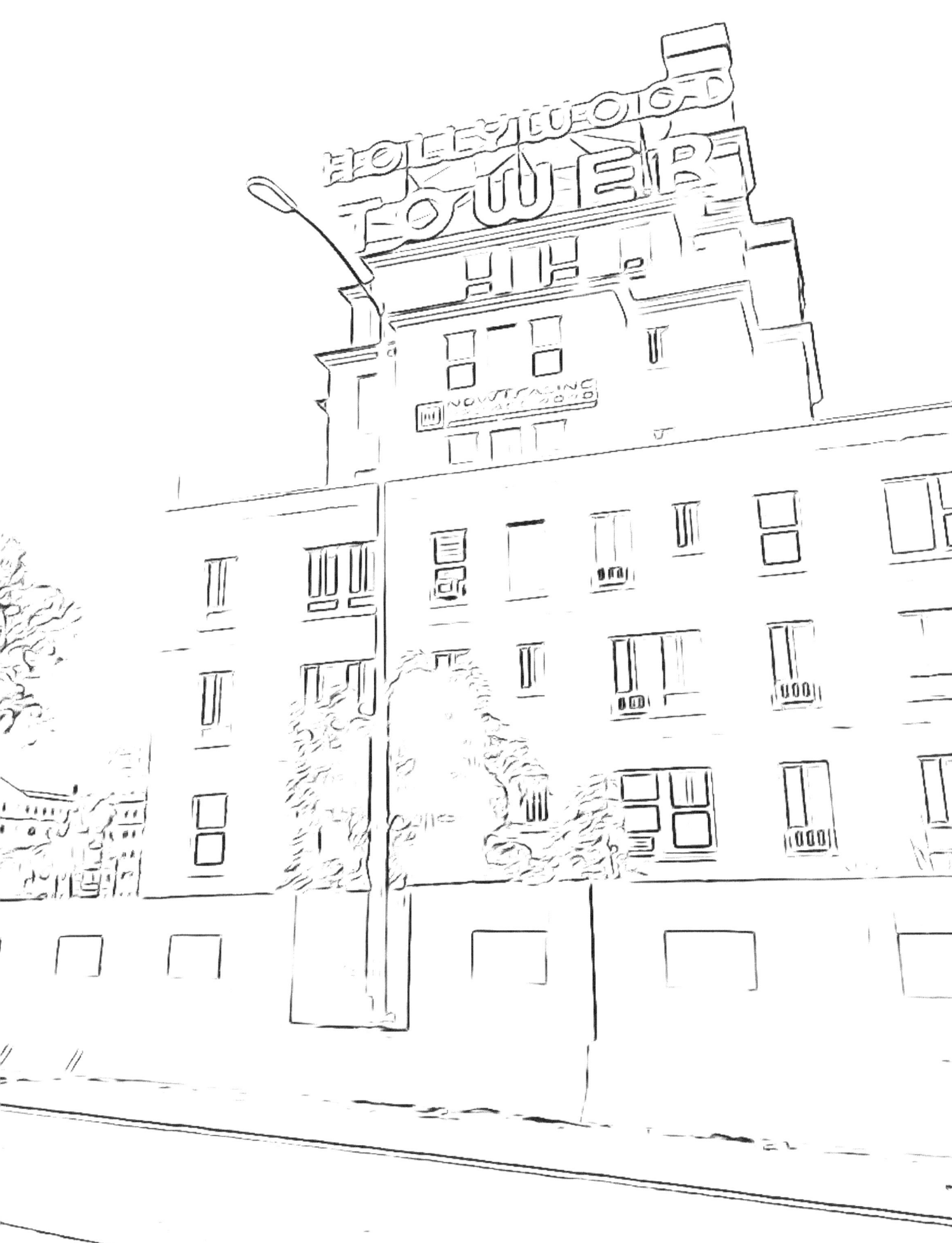

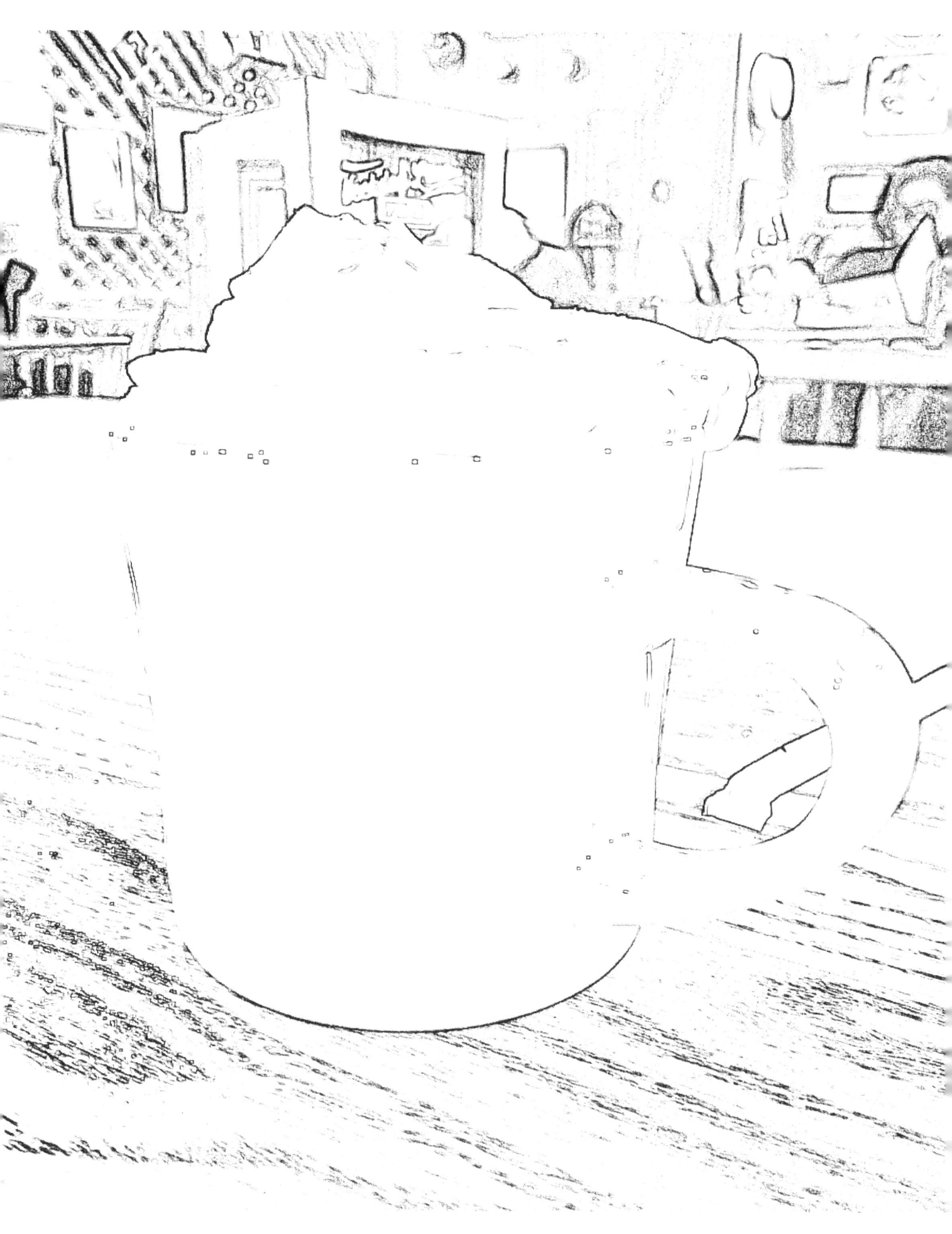

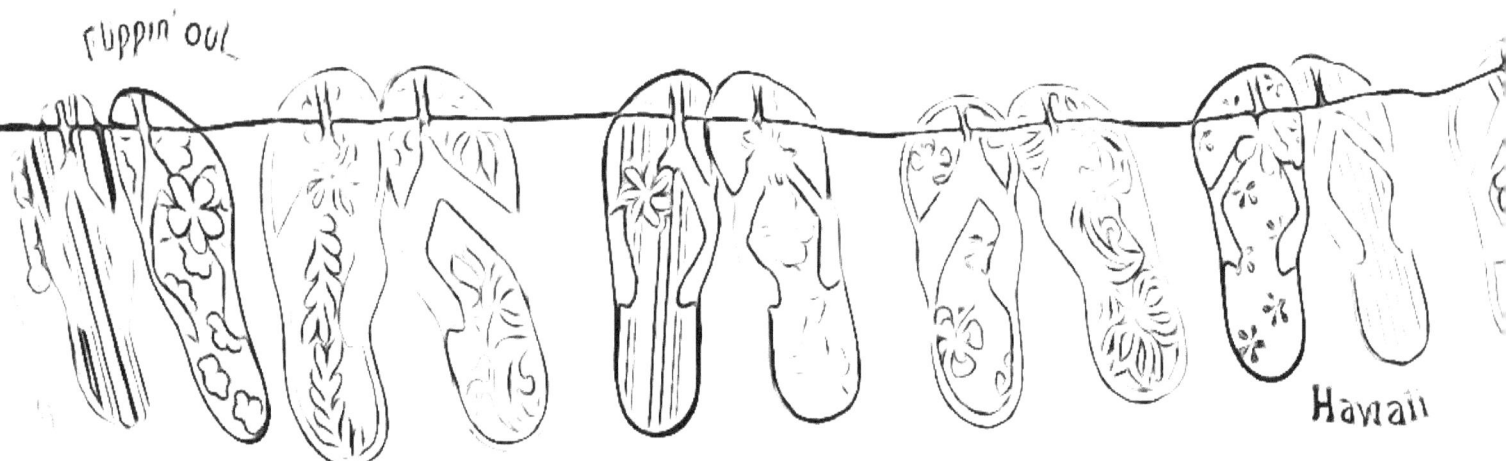

rippin' out

Havraii

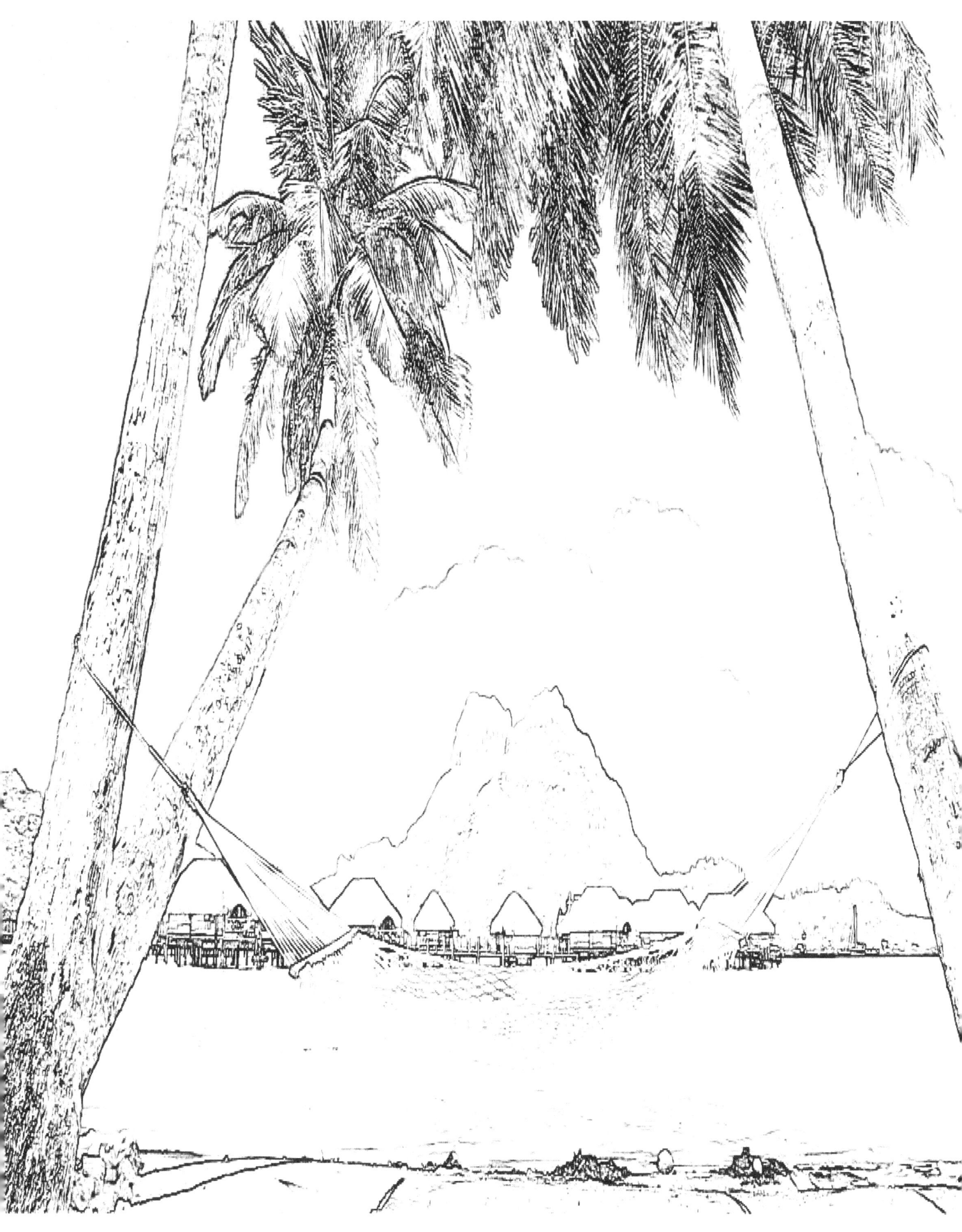

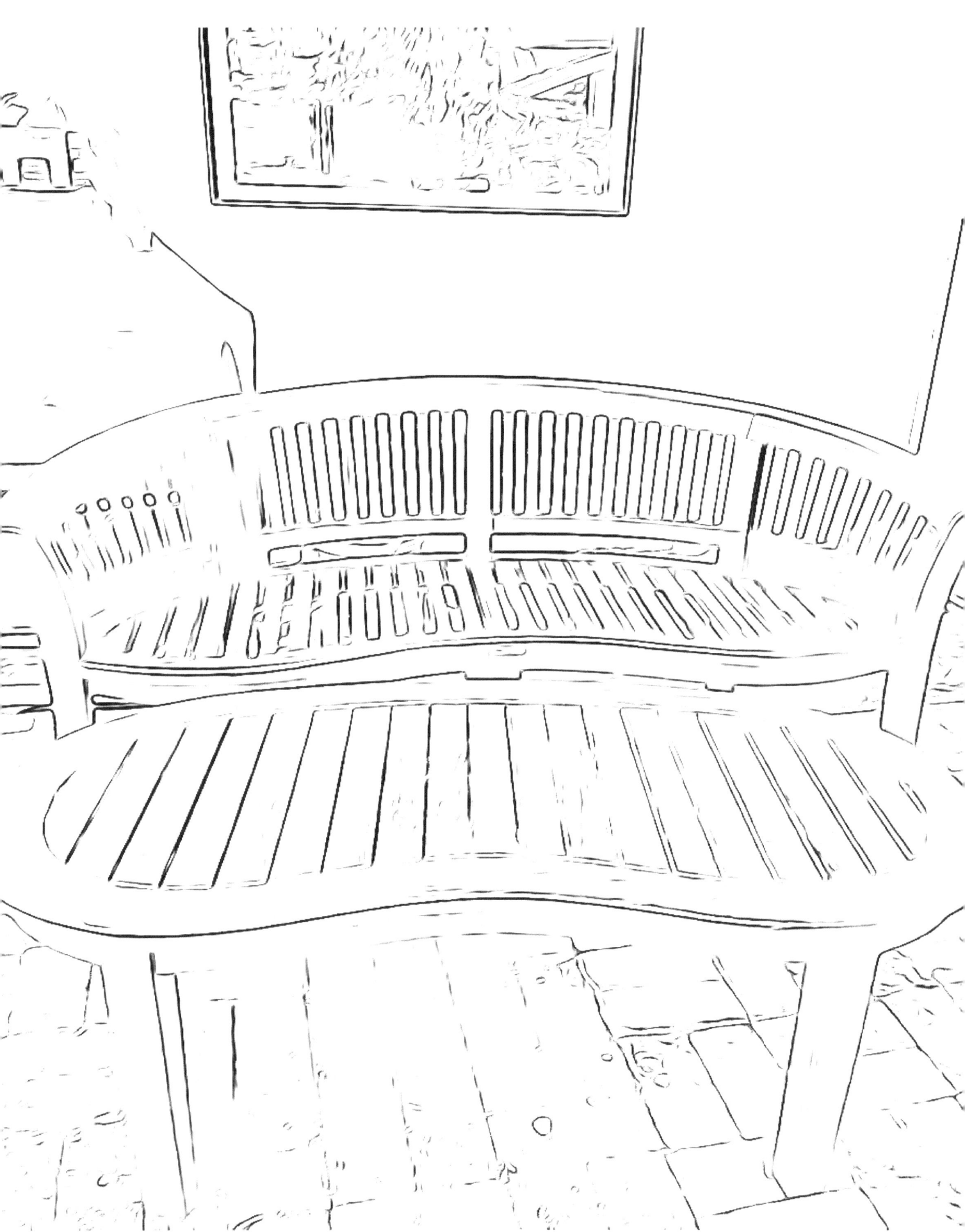

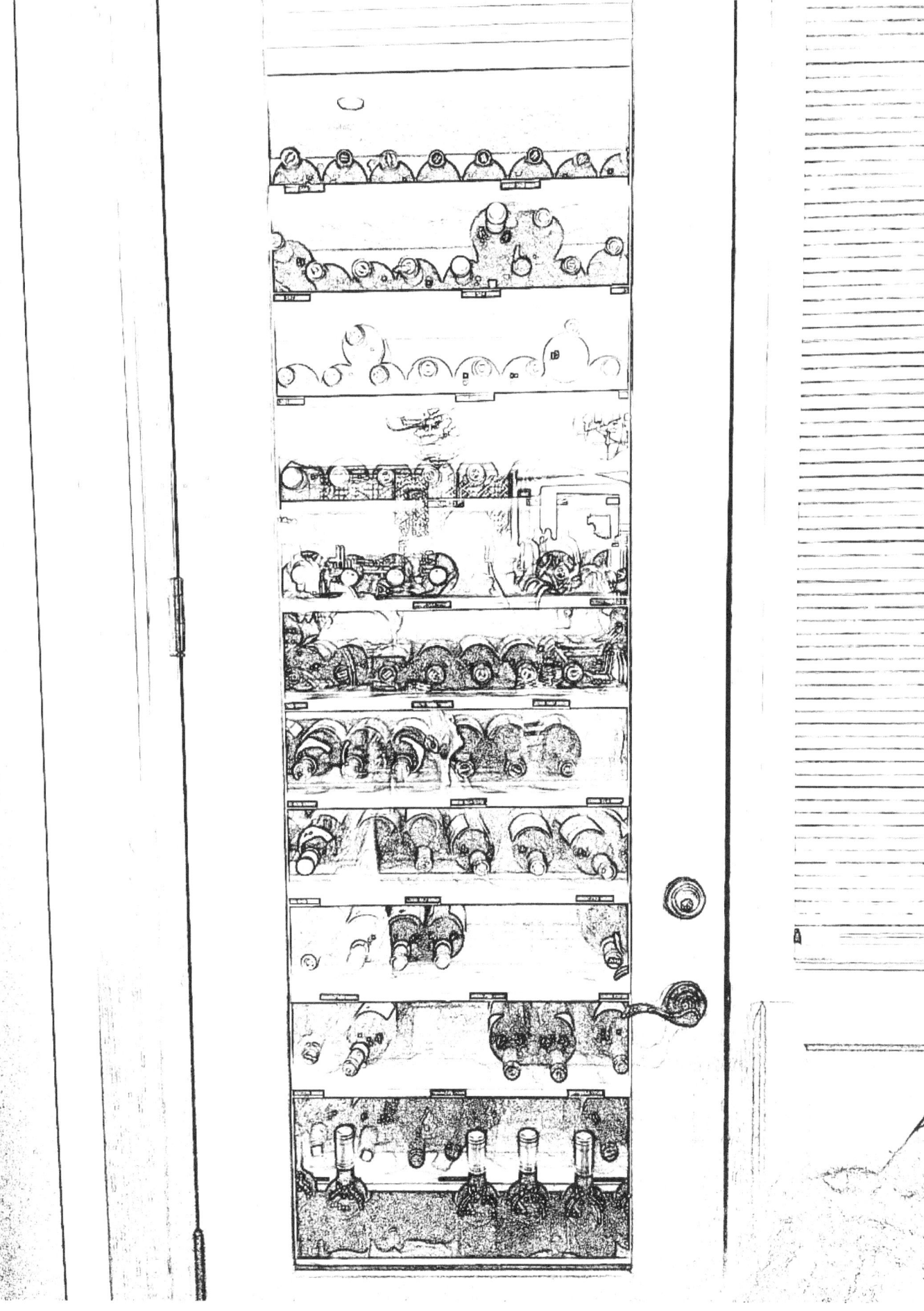

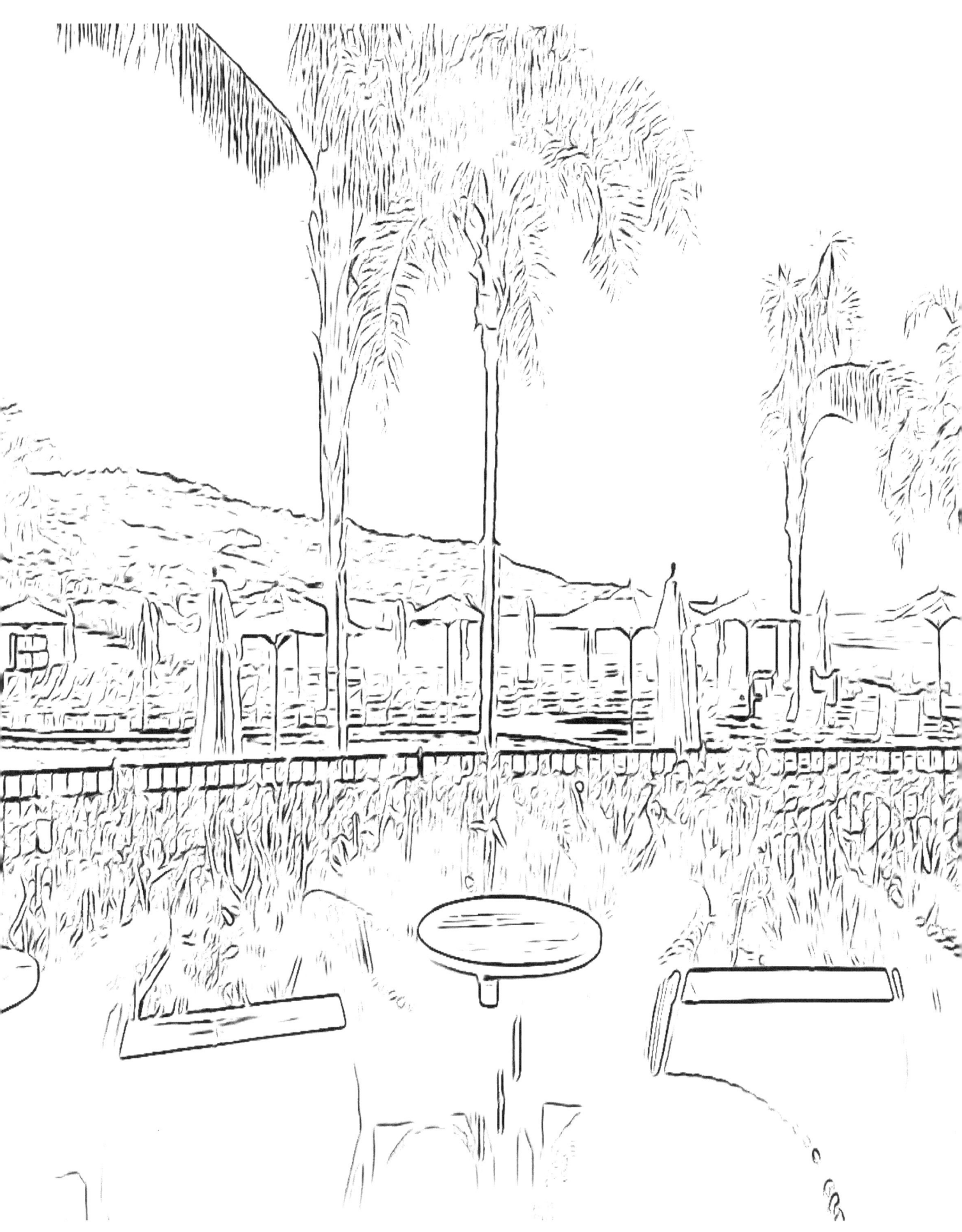

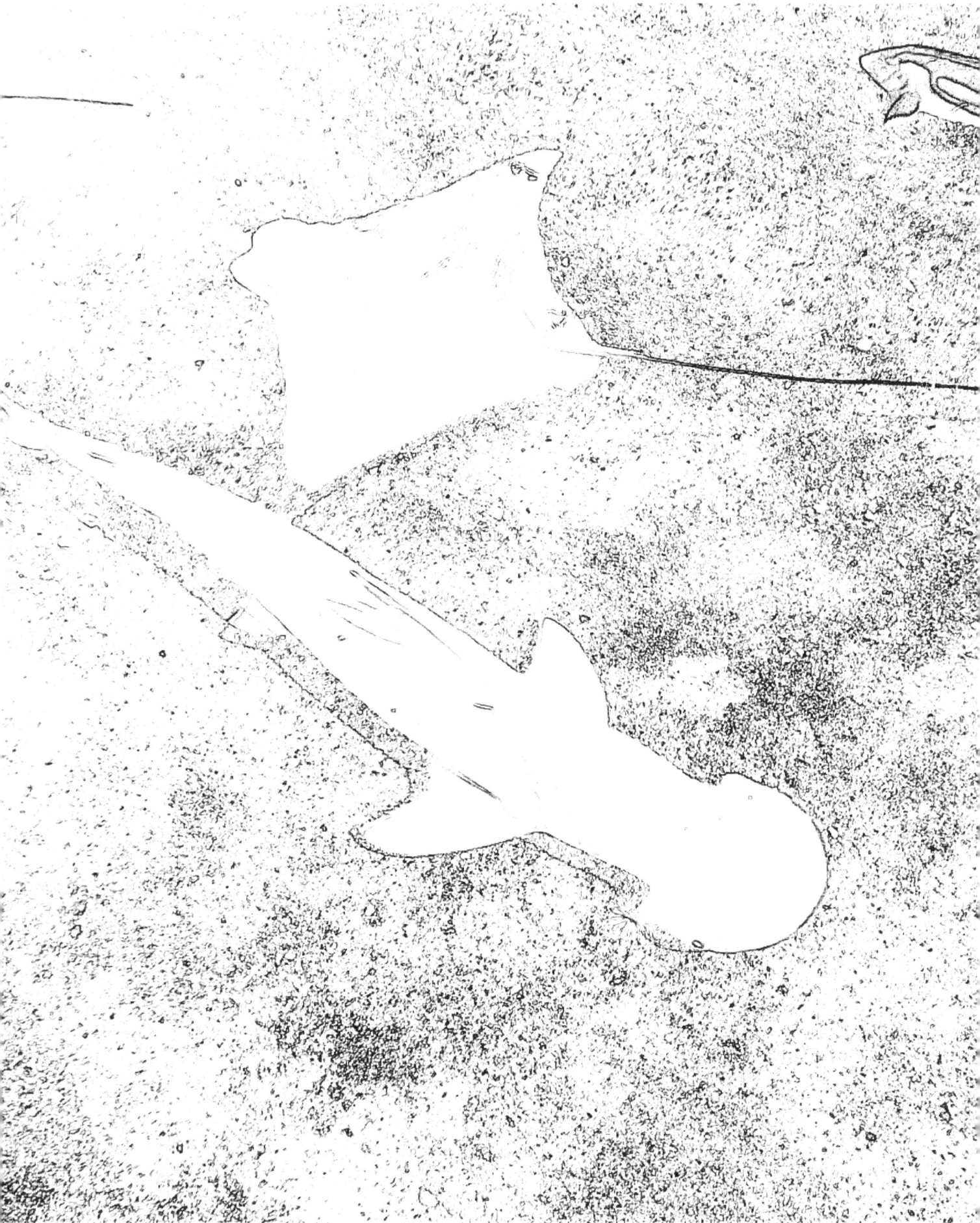

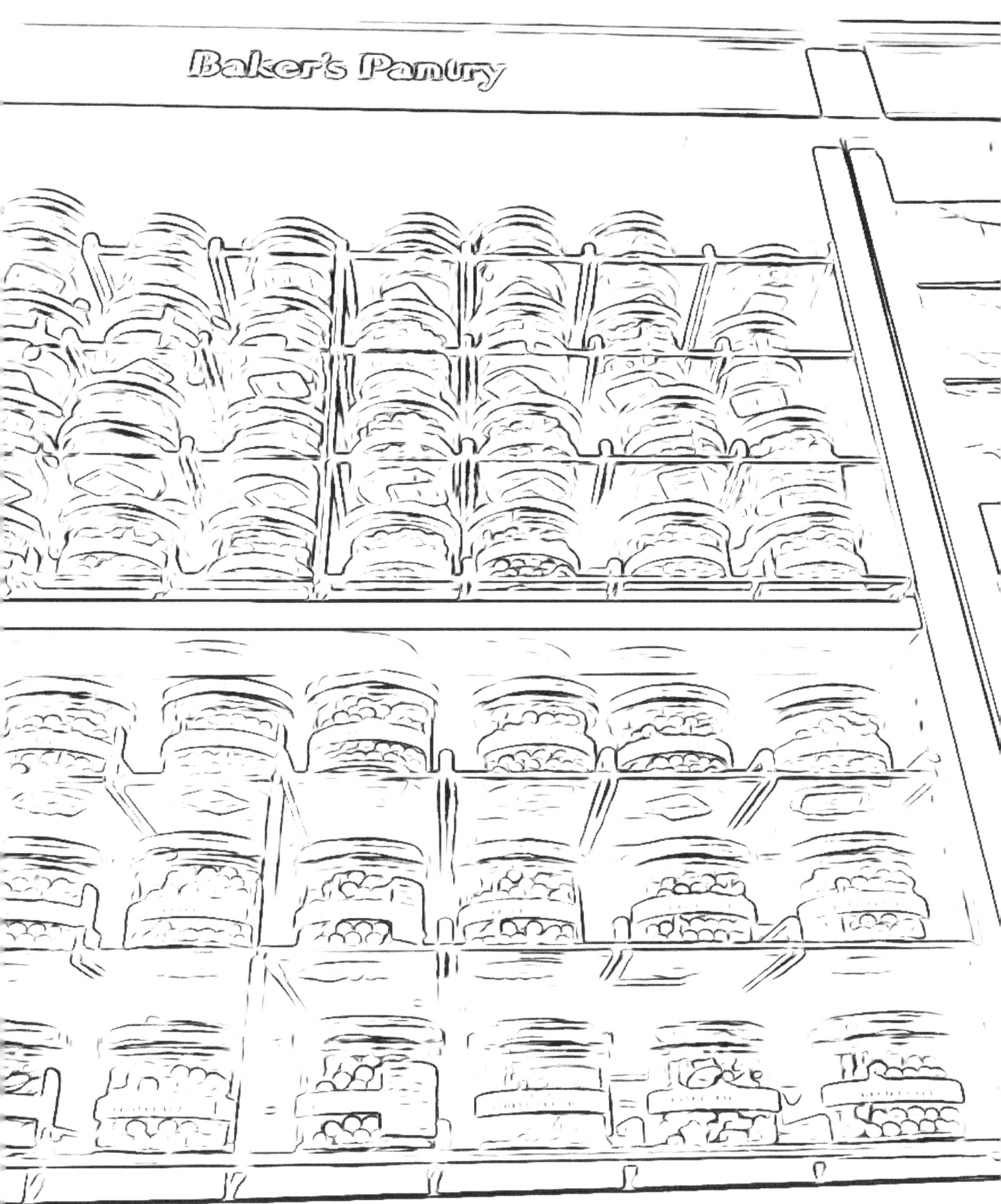

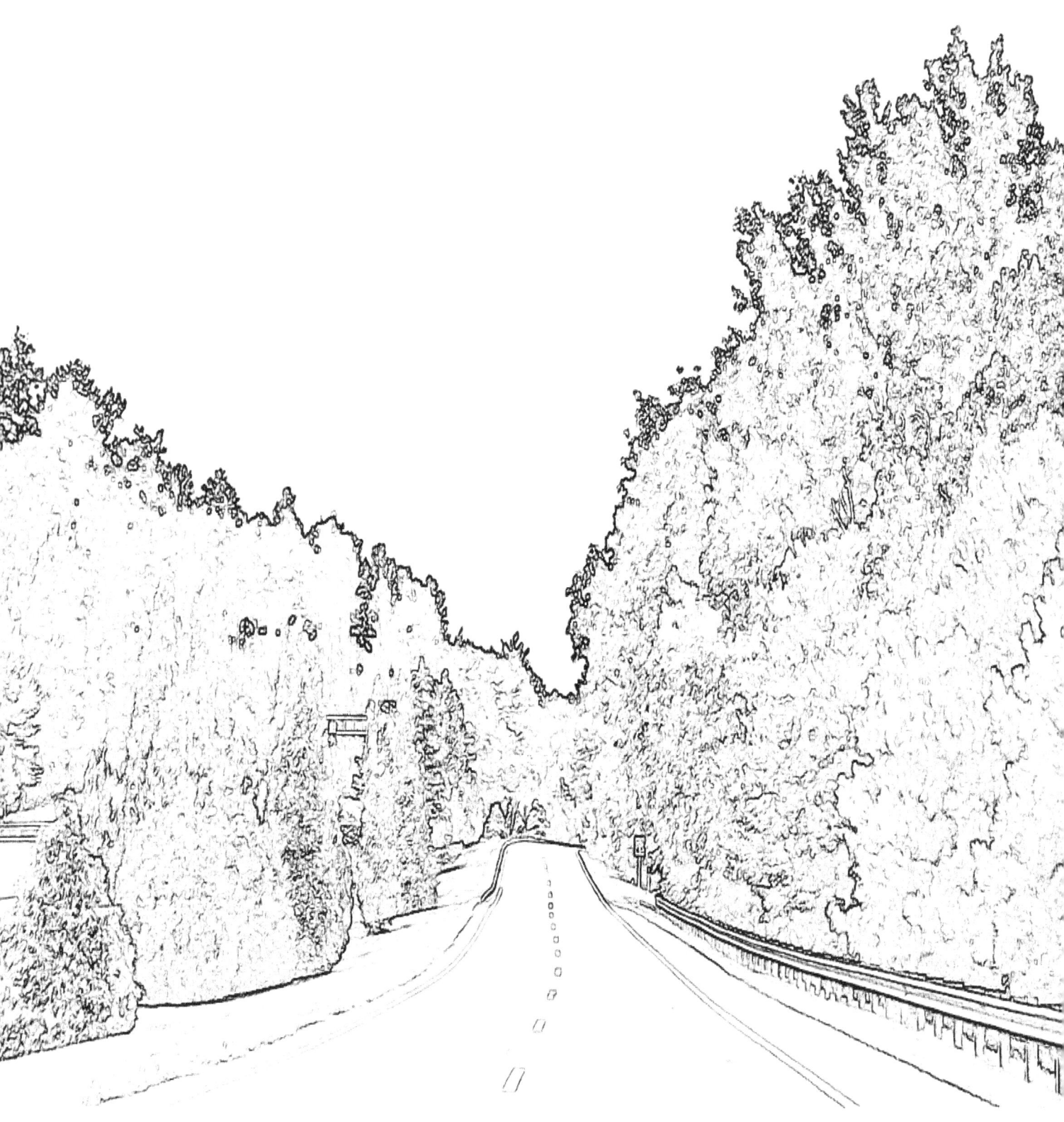

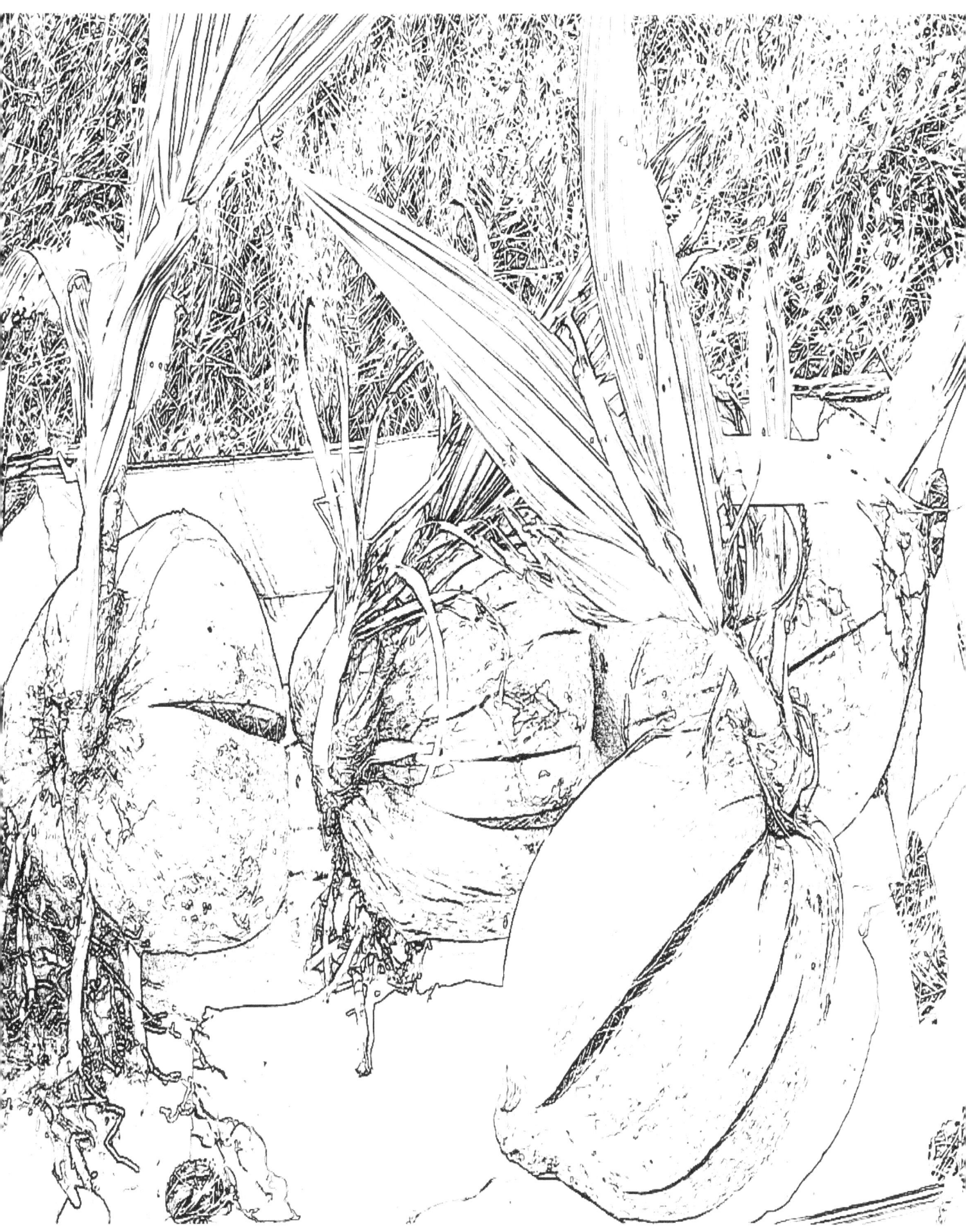

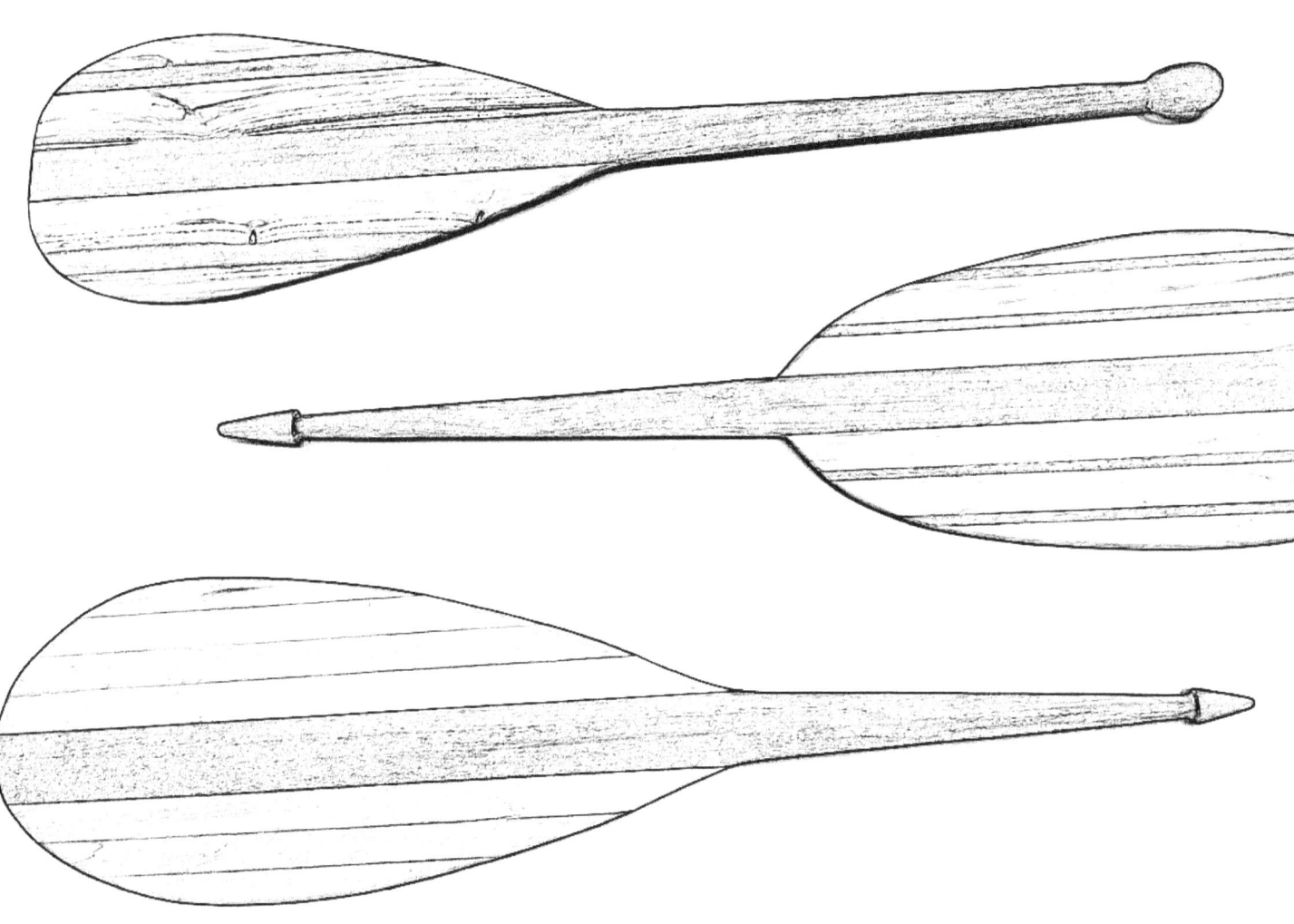

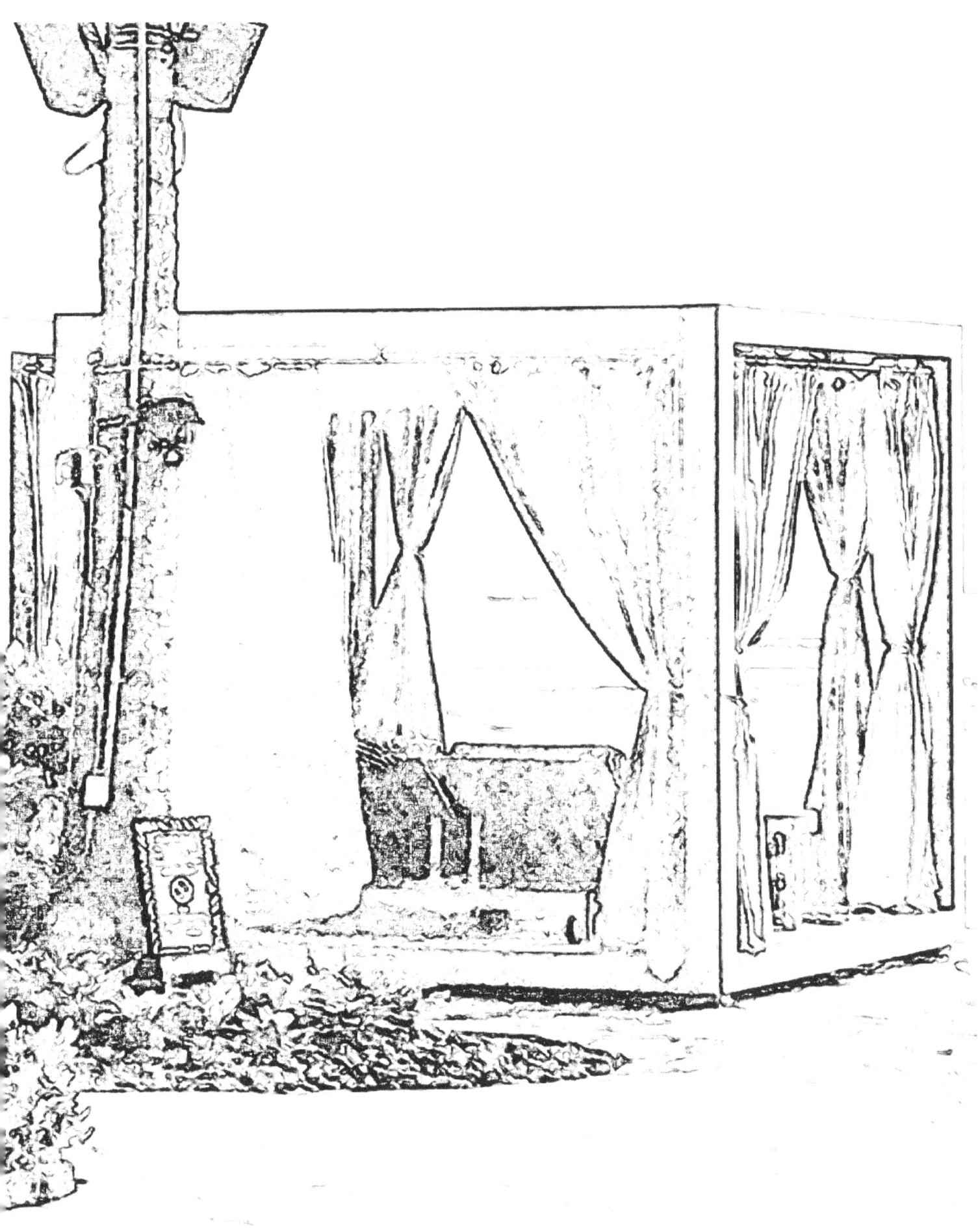

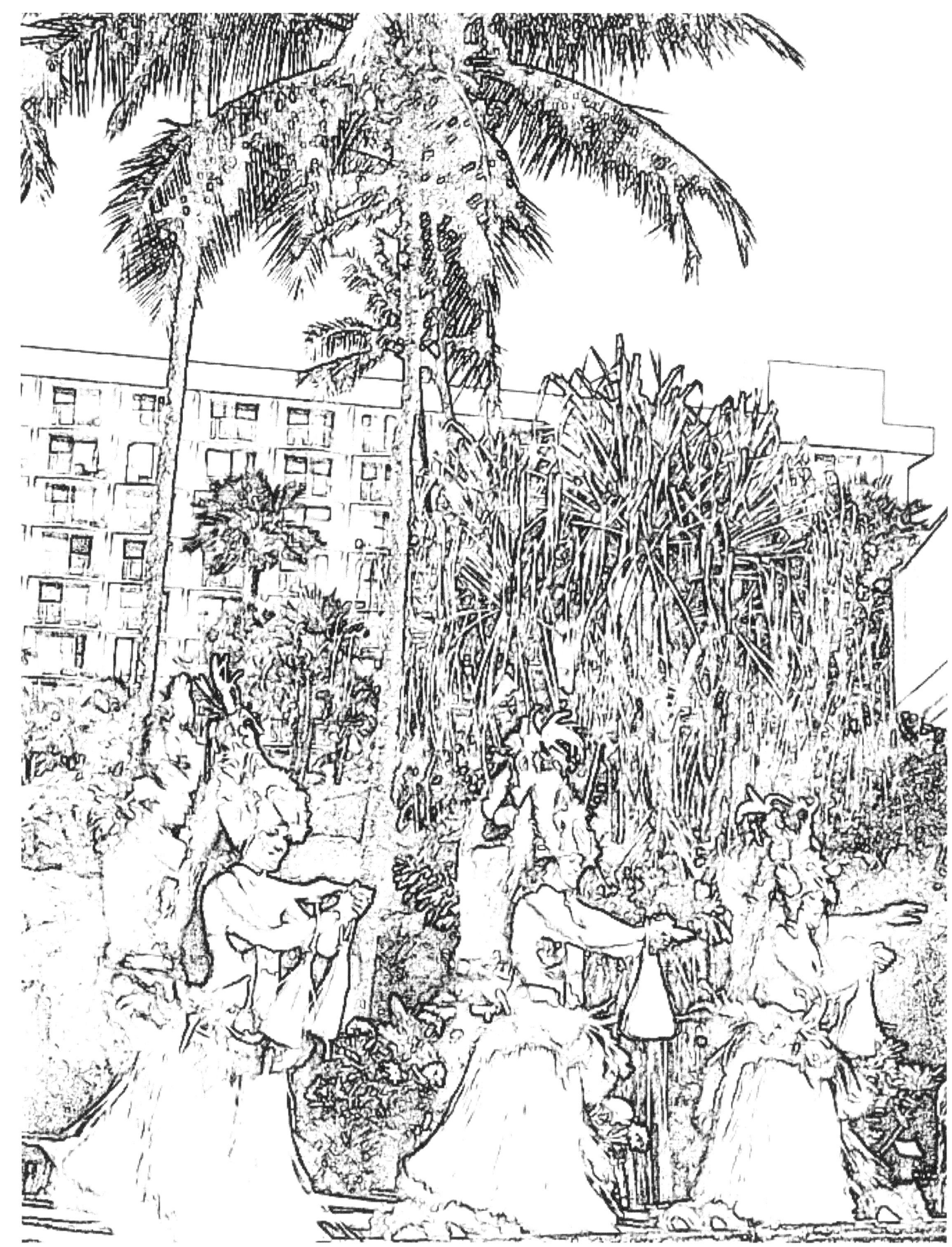

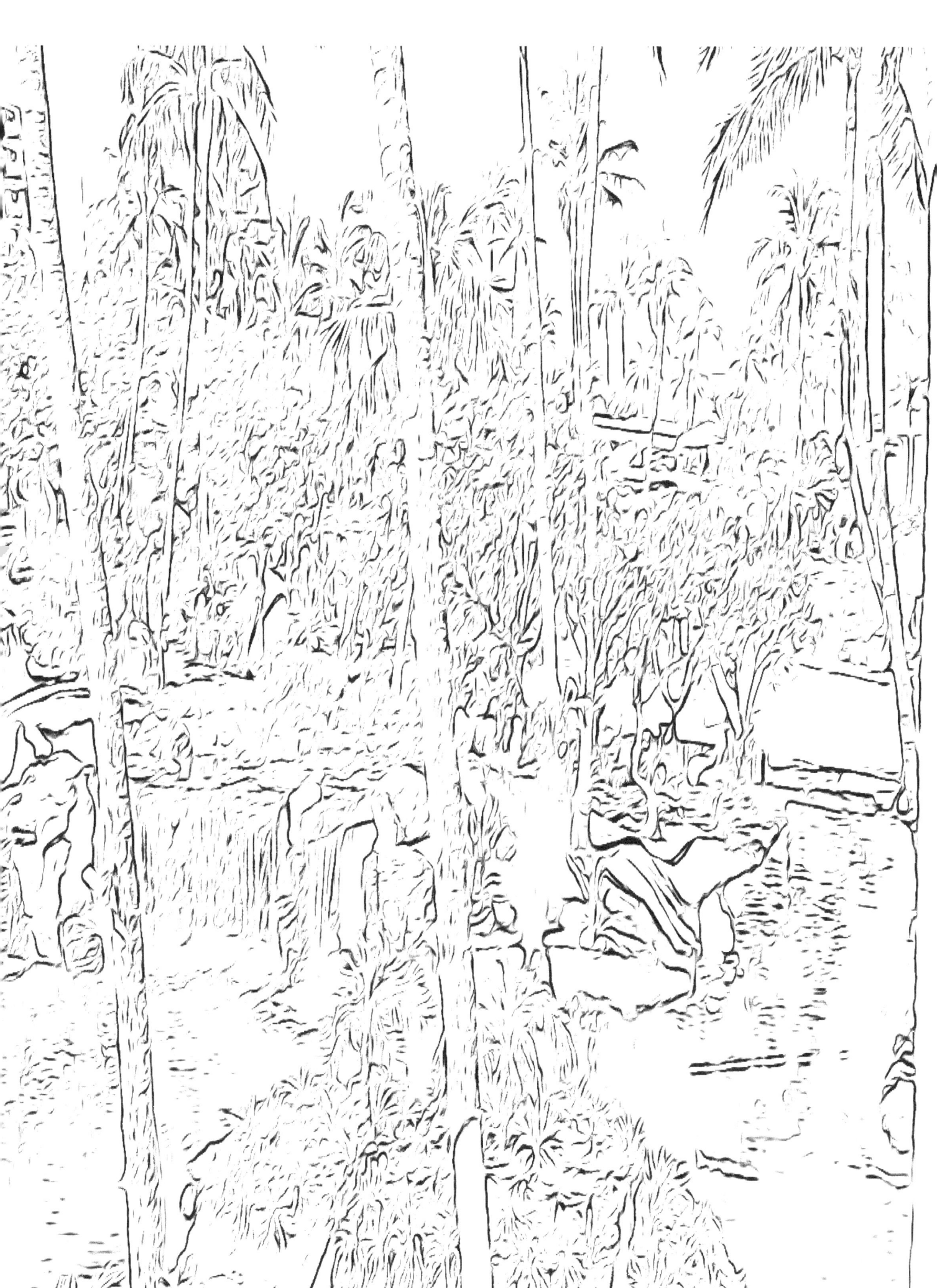

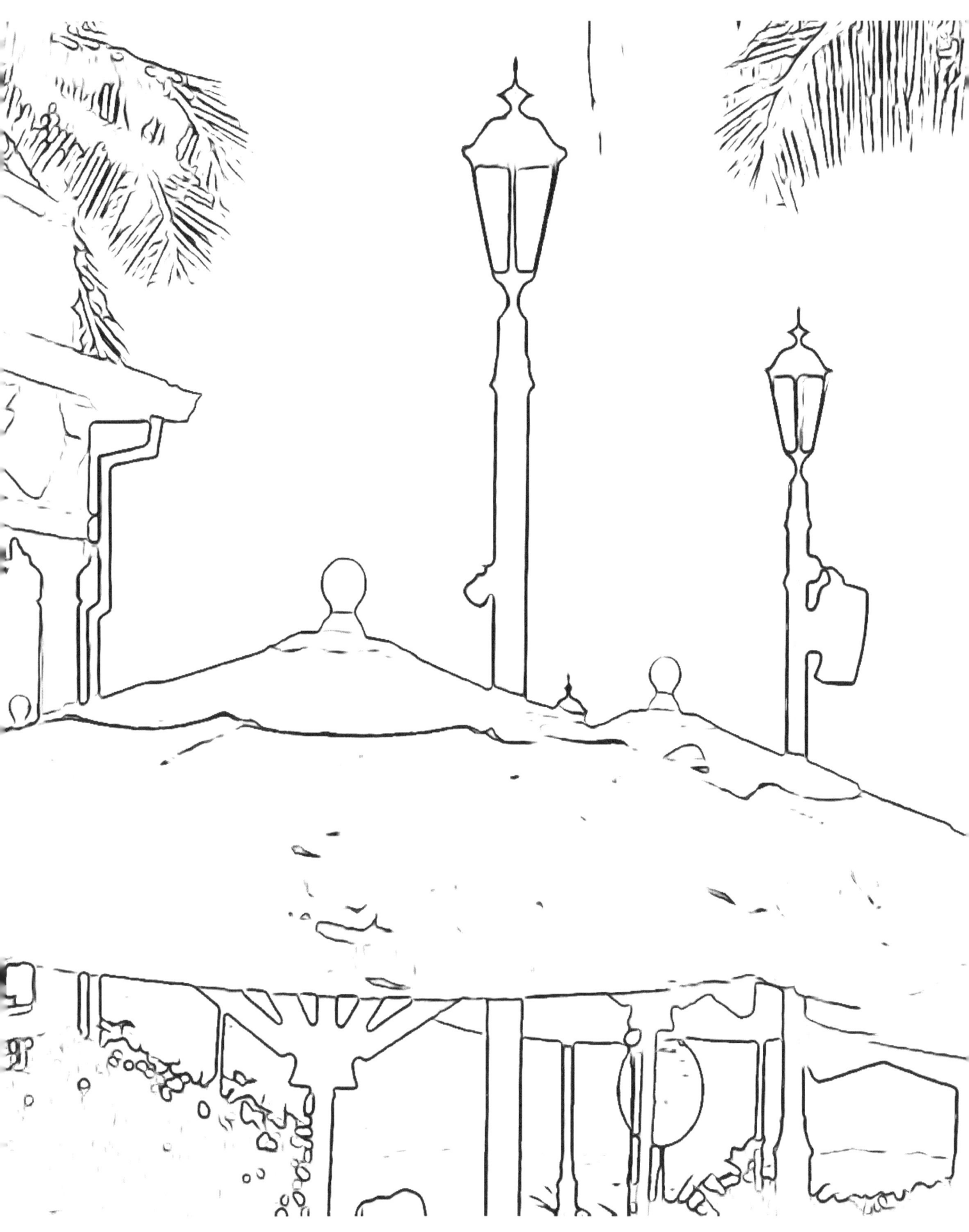

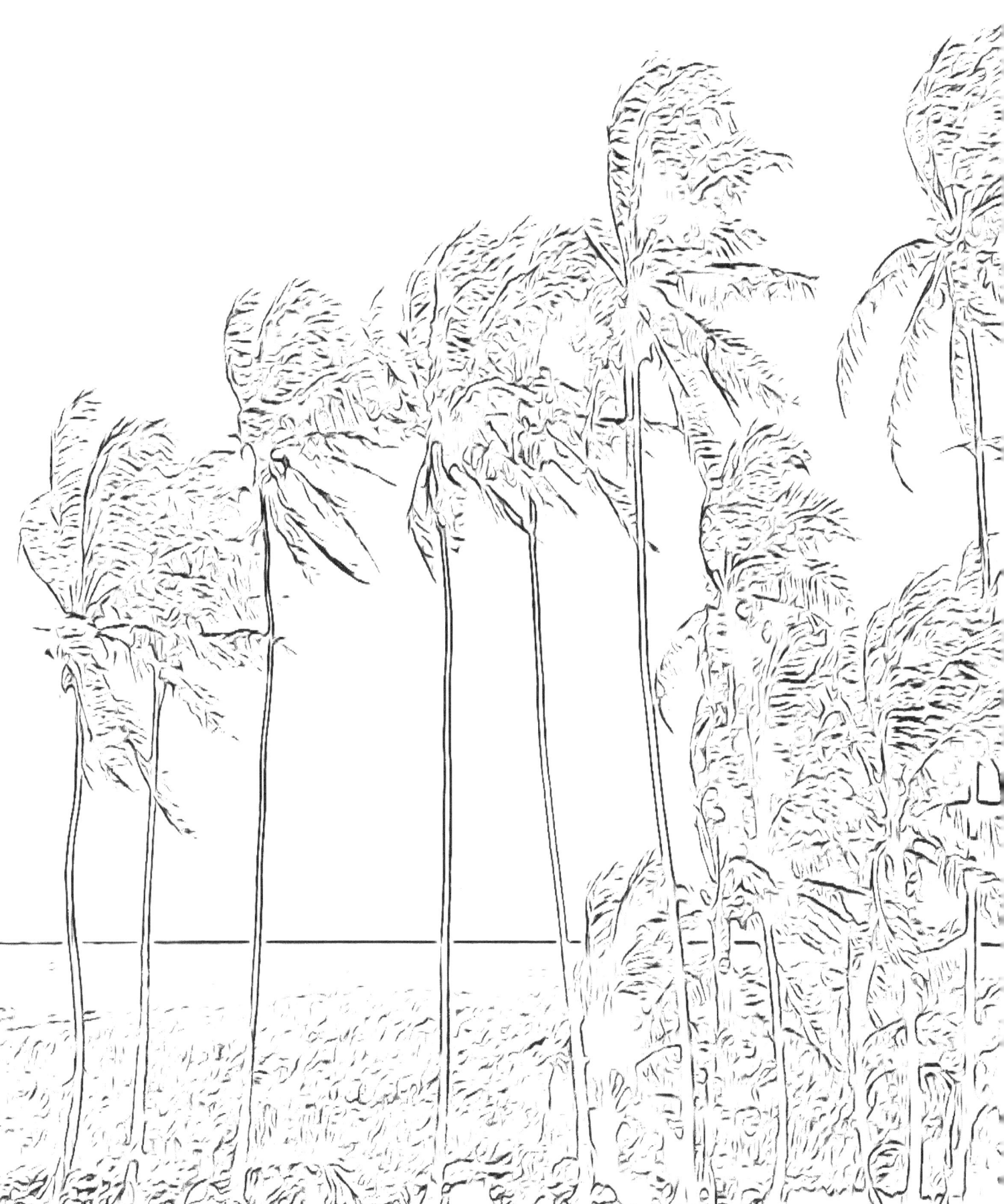

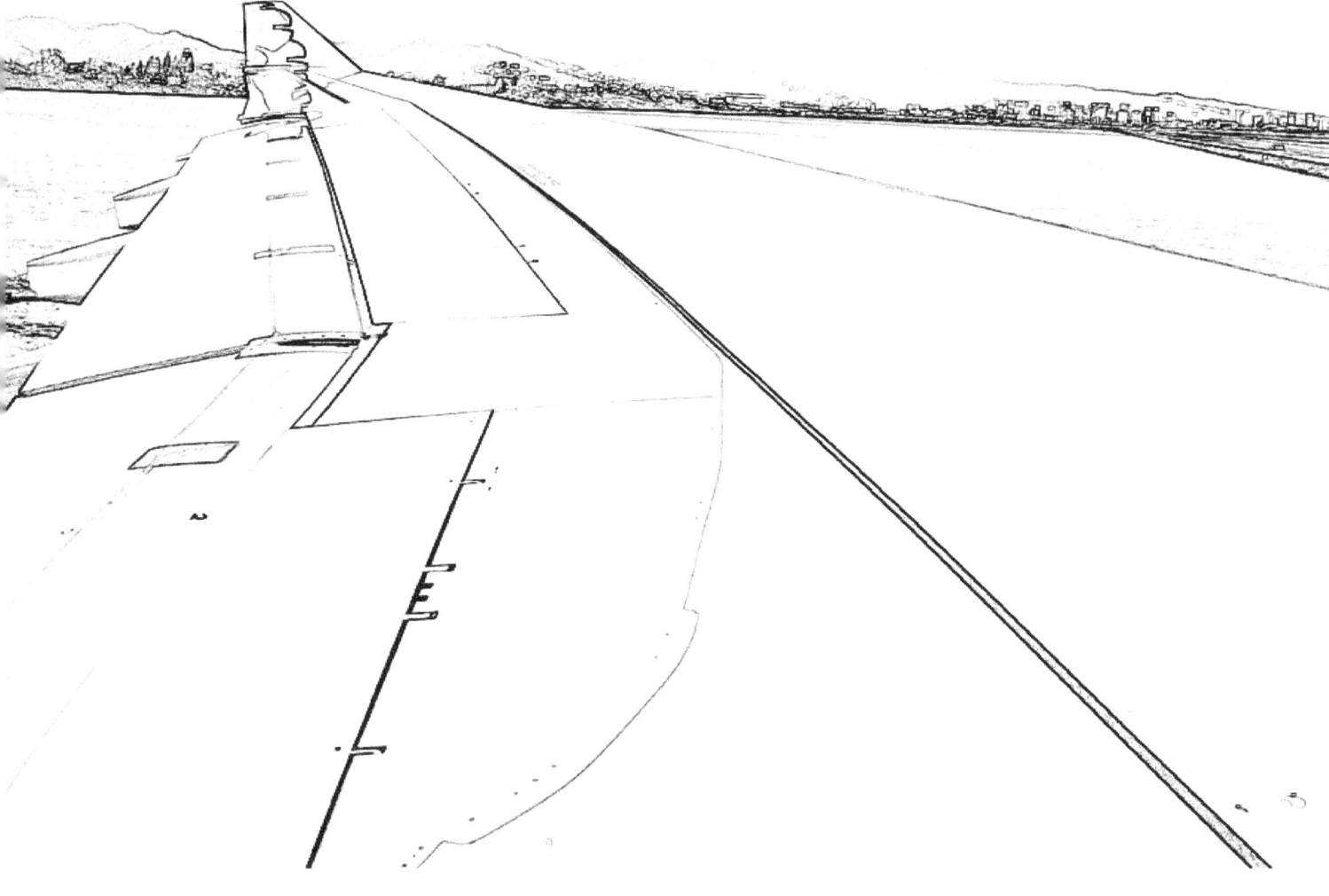

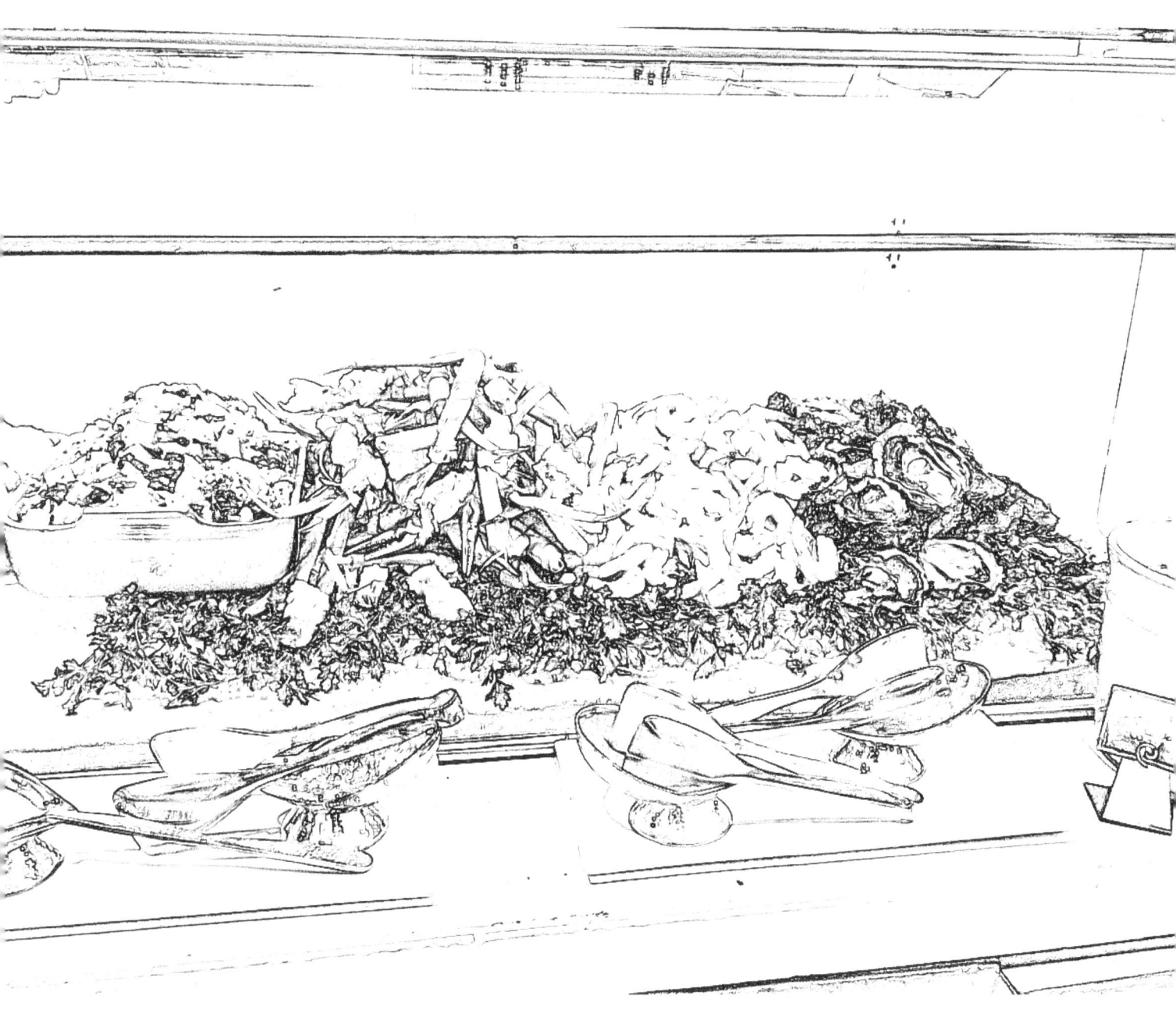

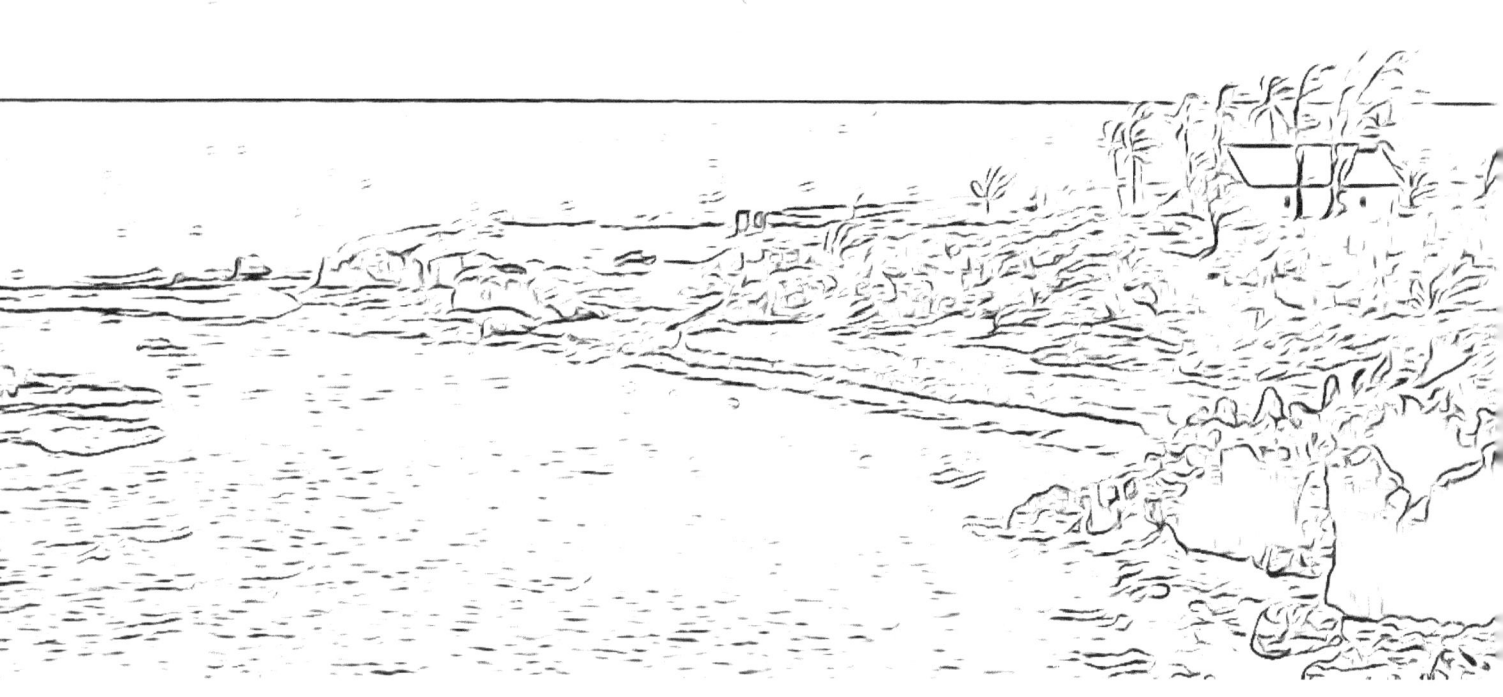

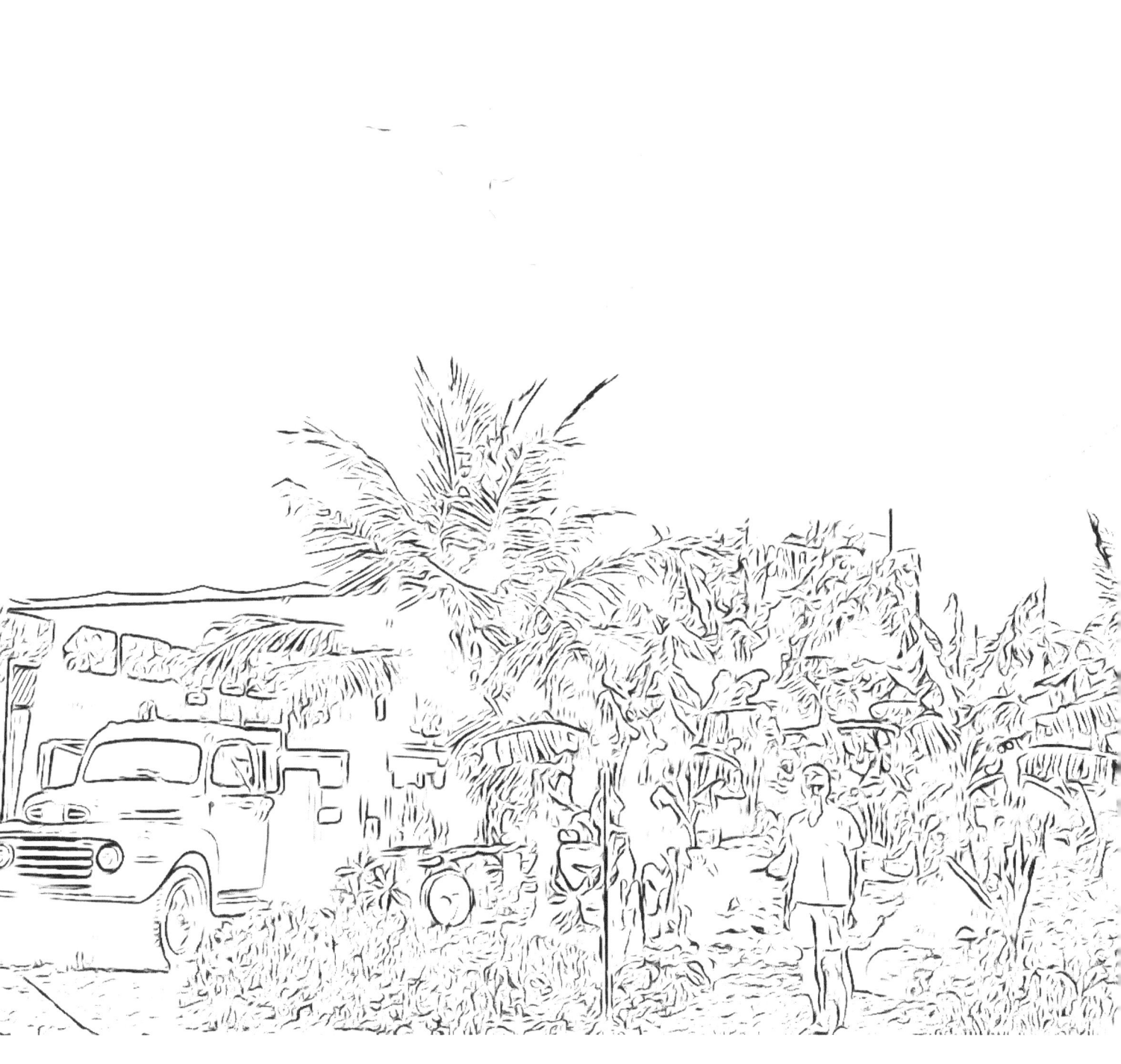

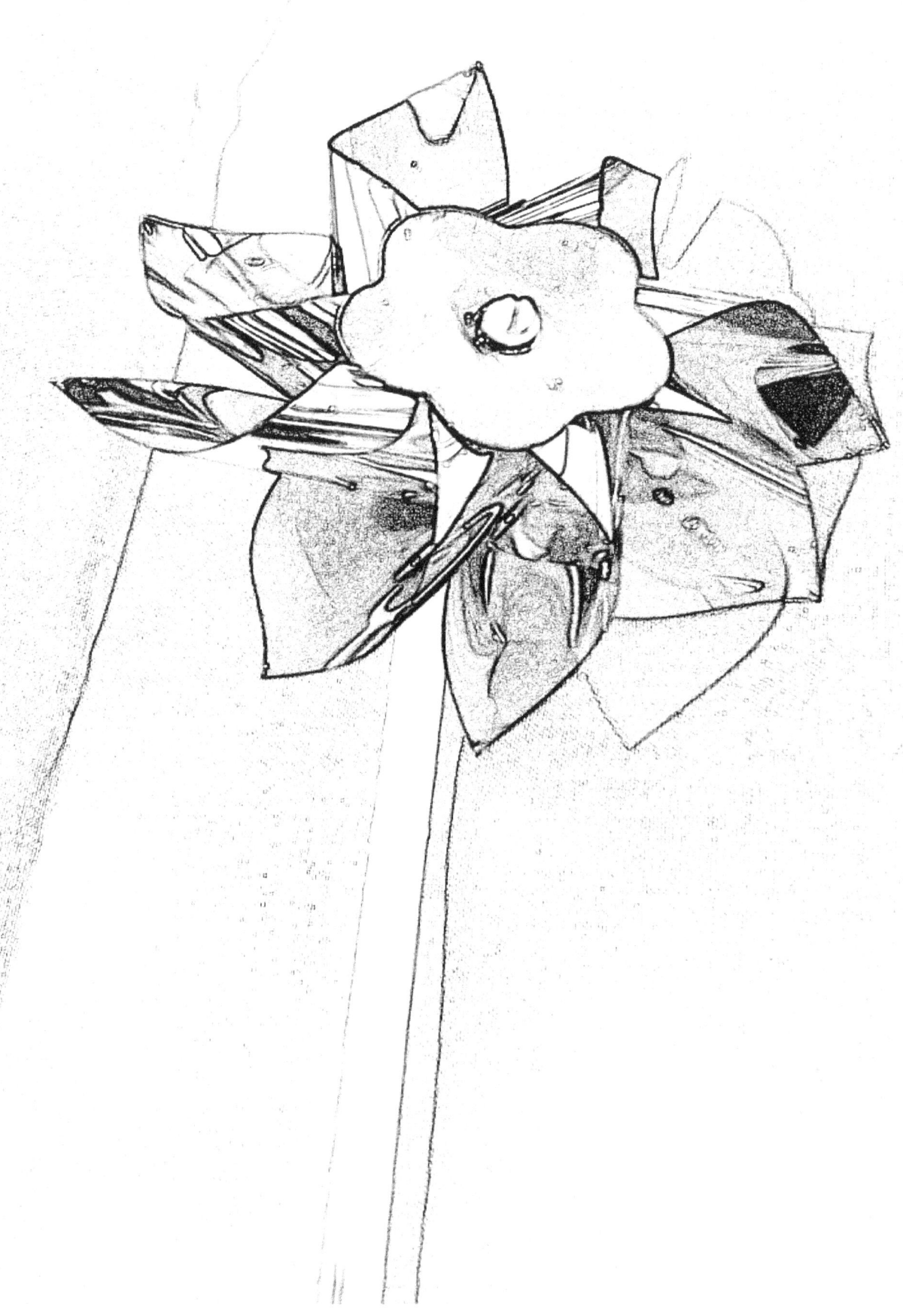

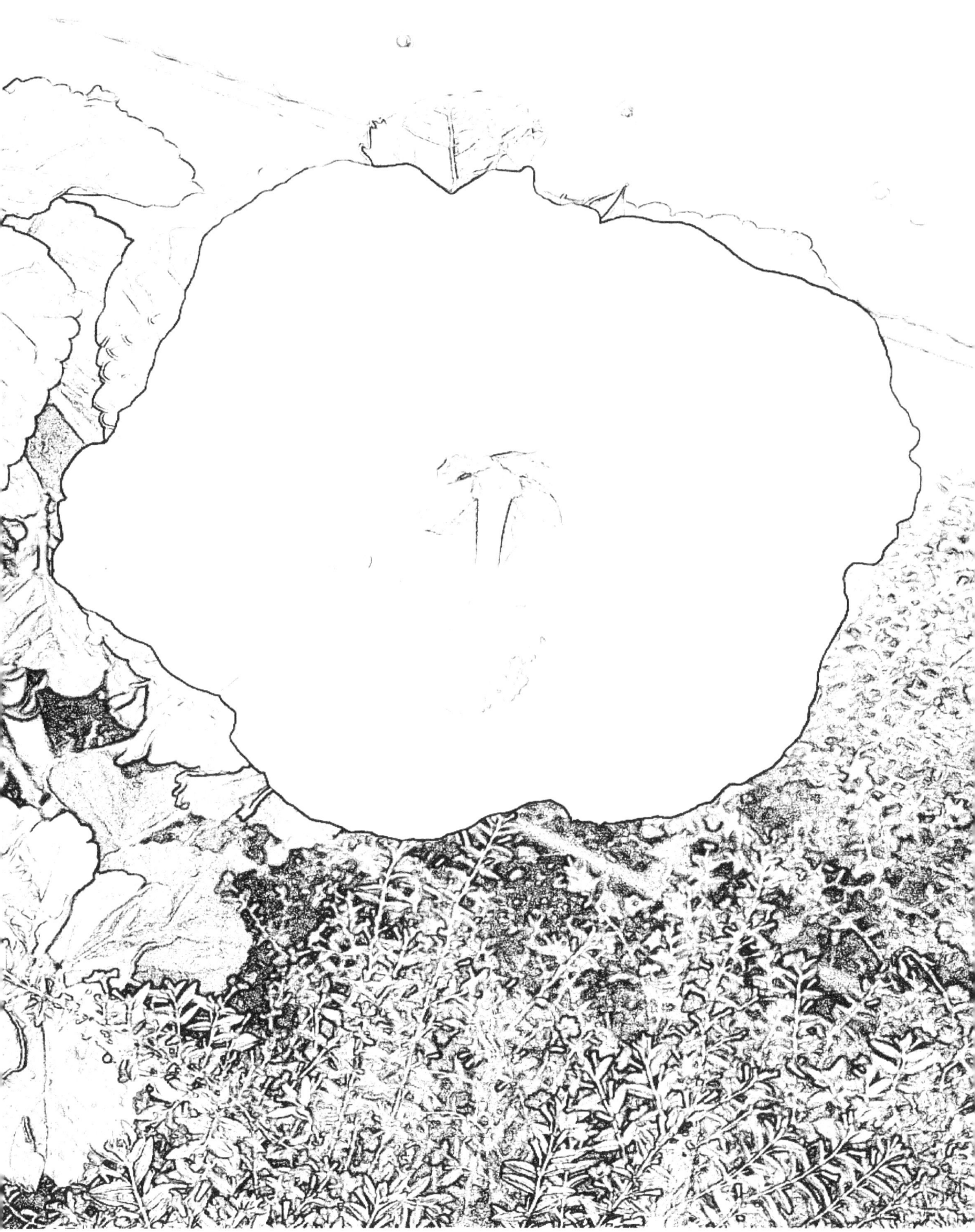

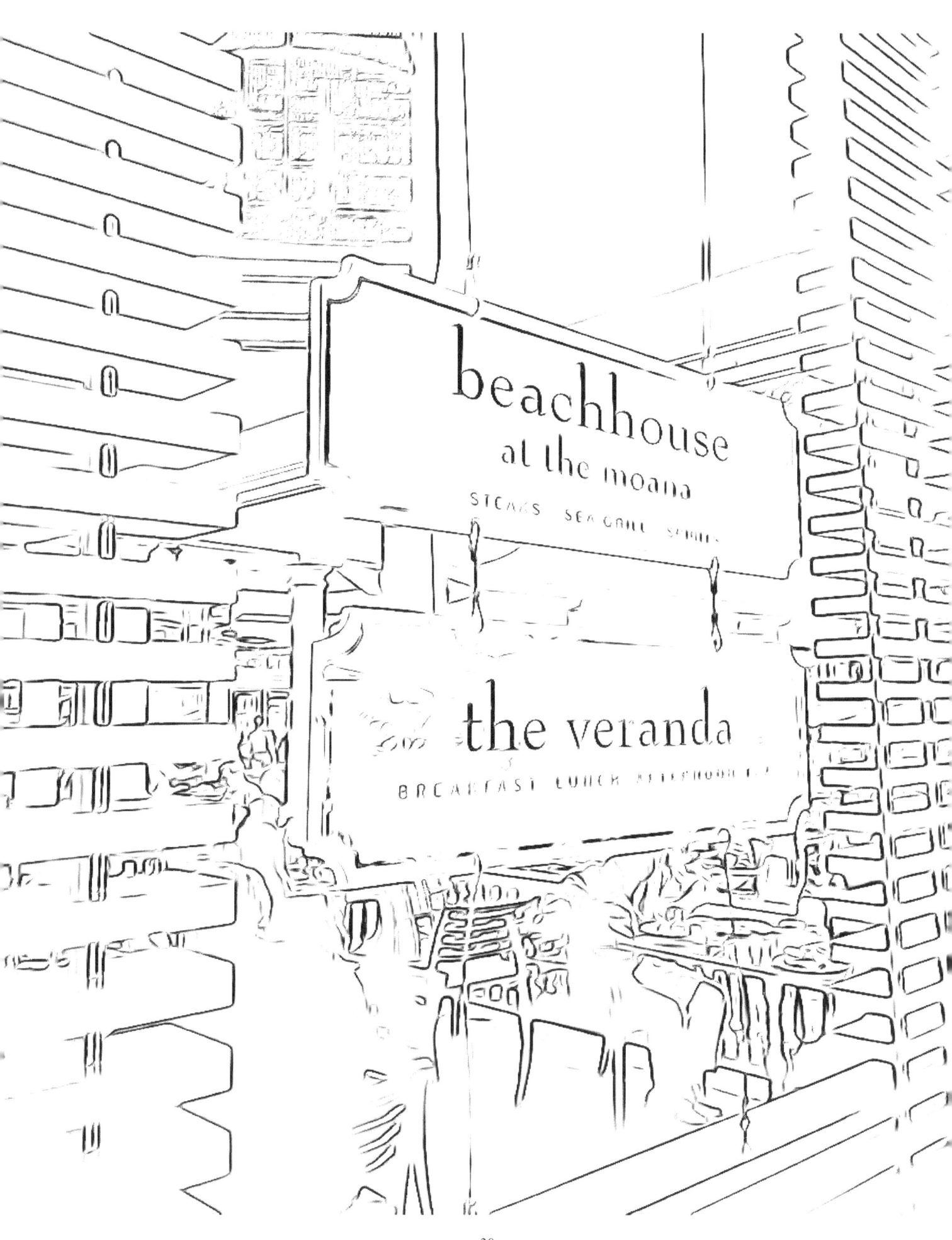

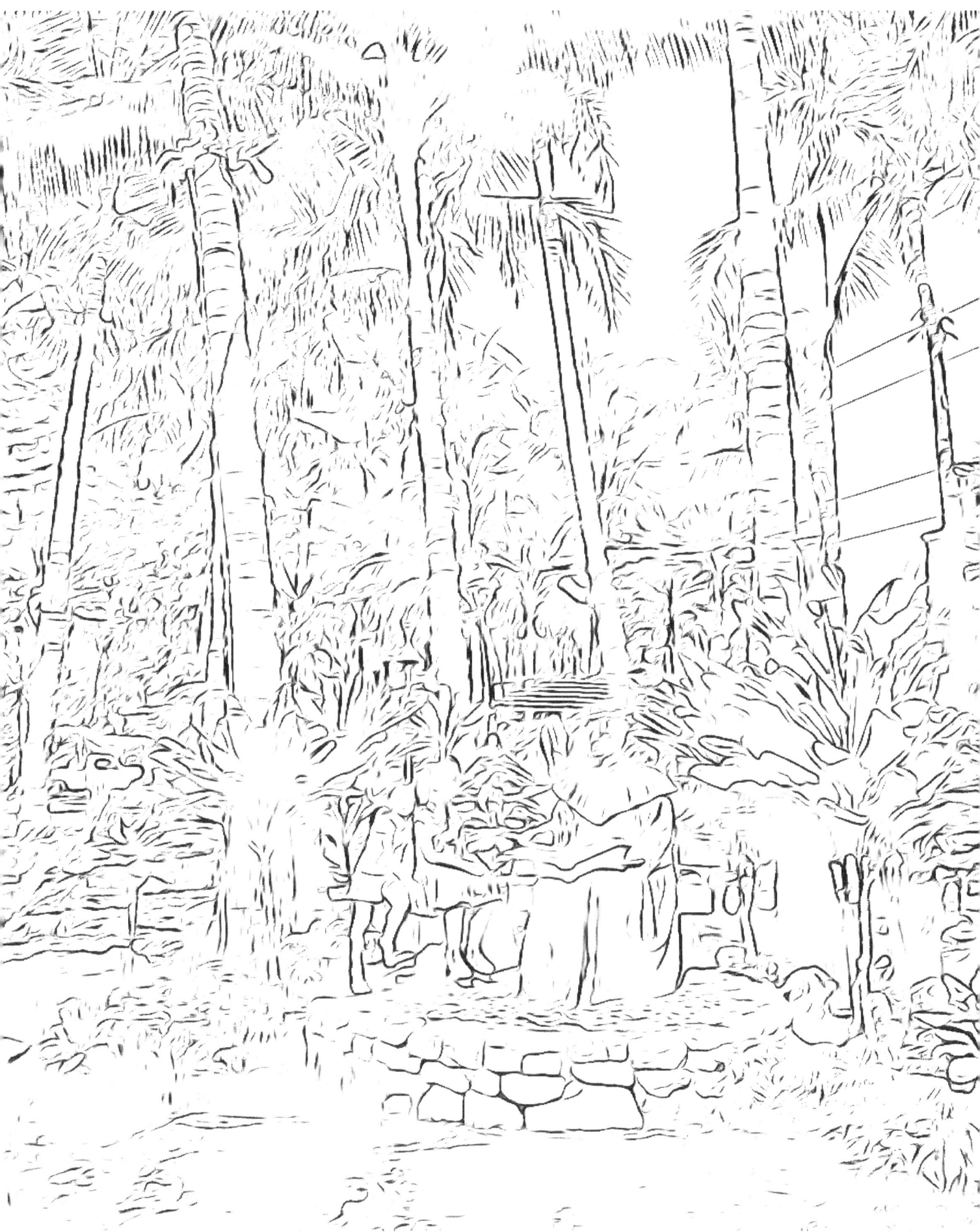

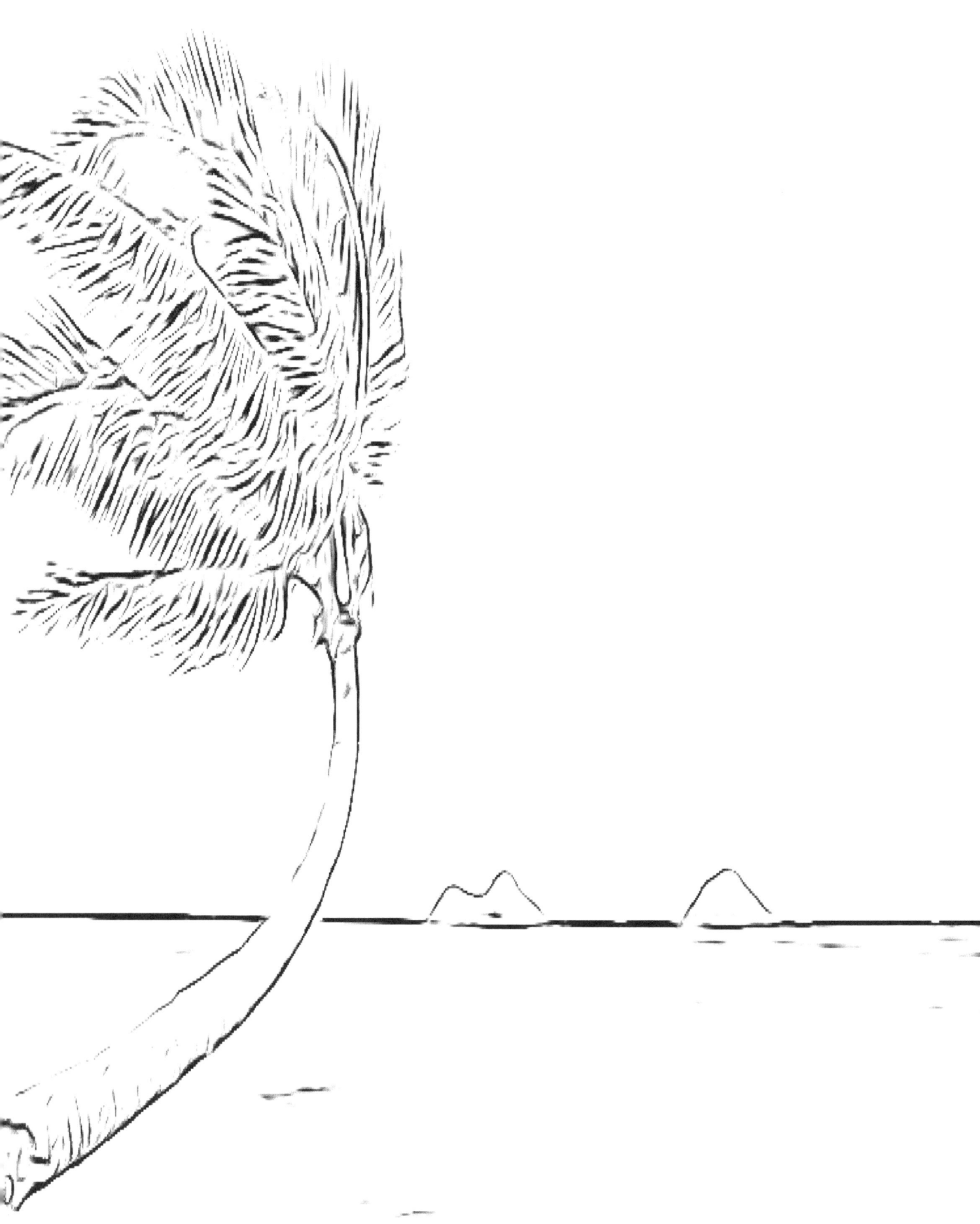

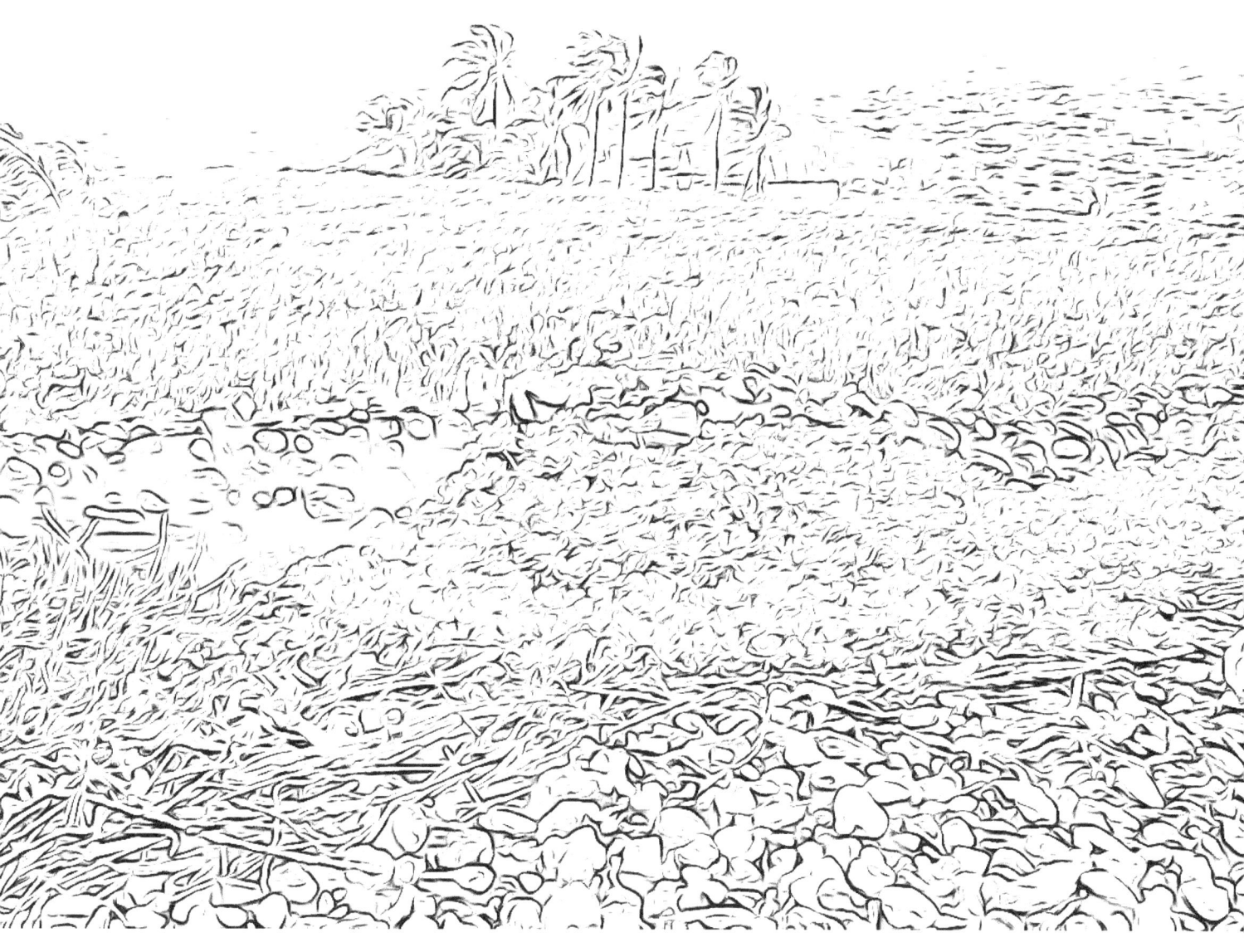

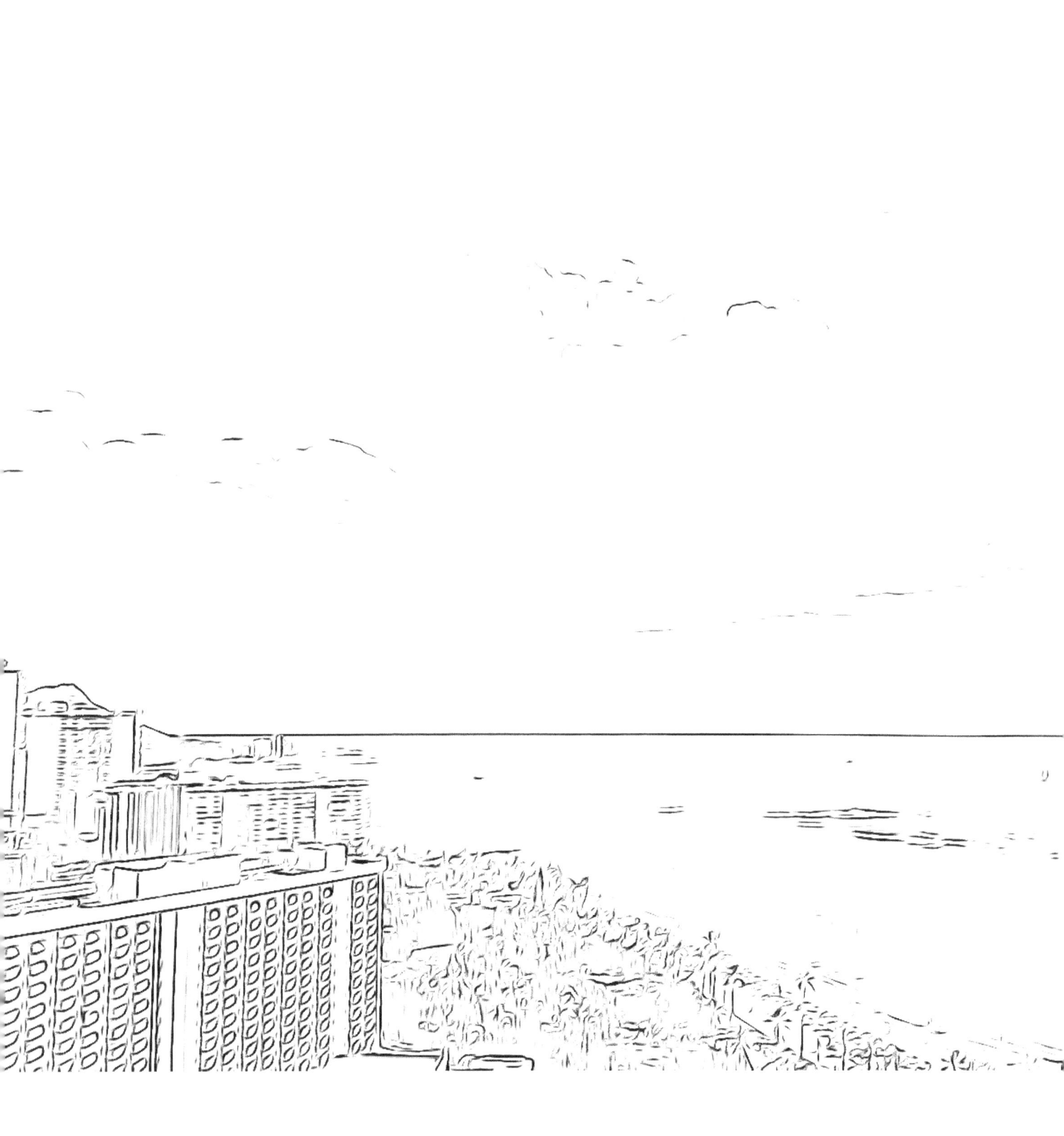

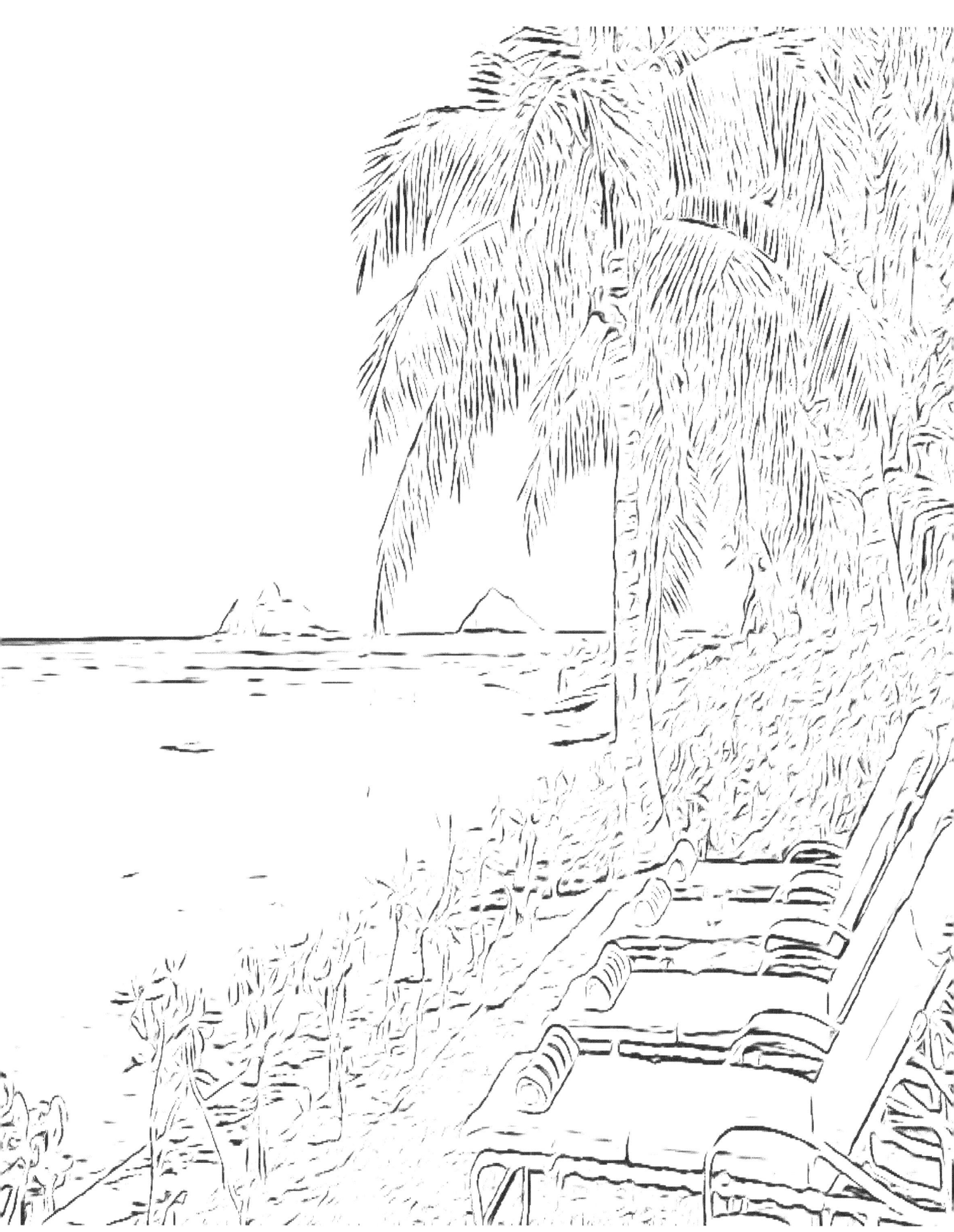

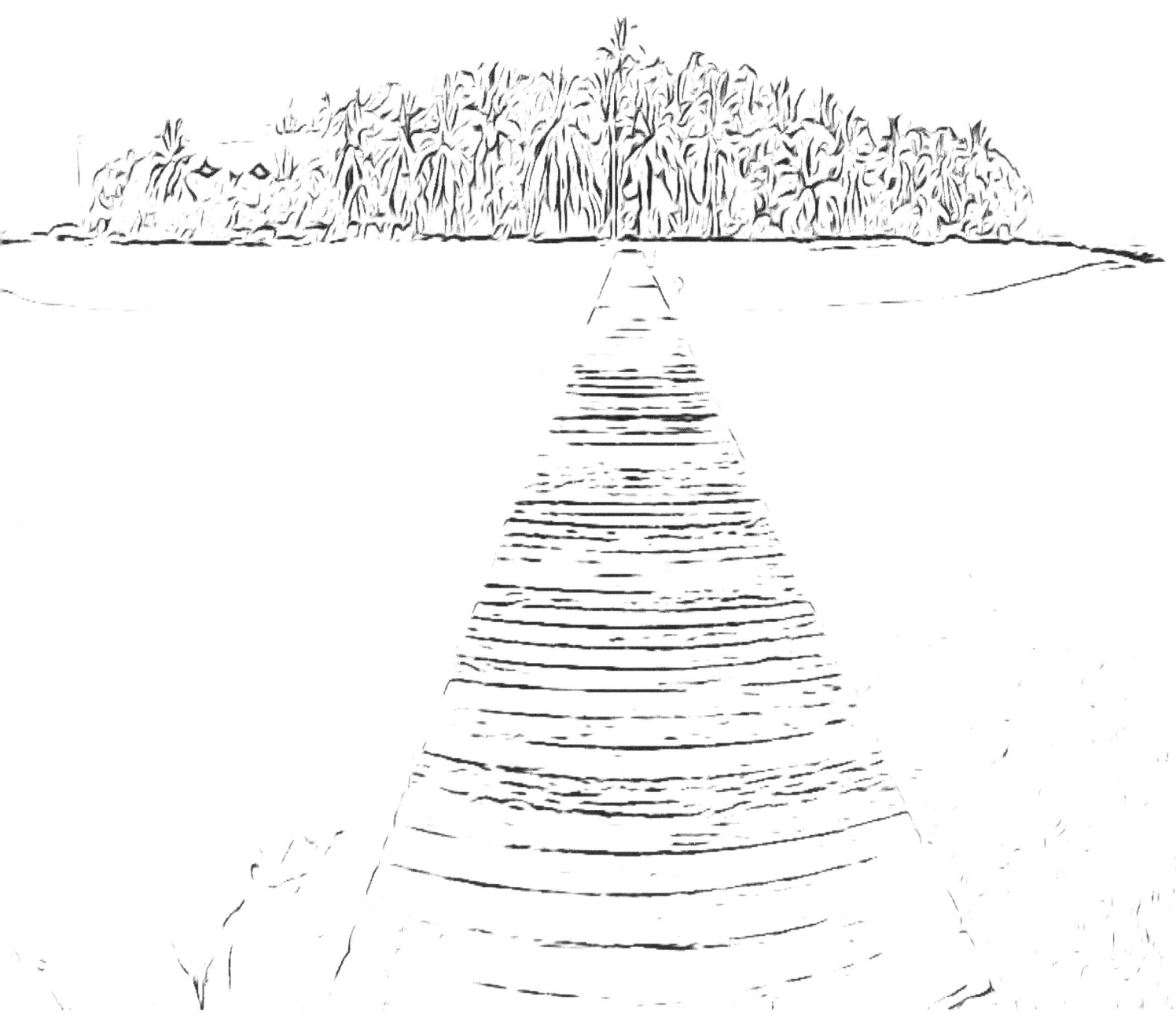

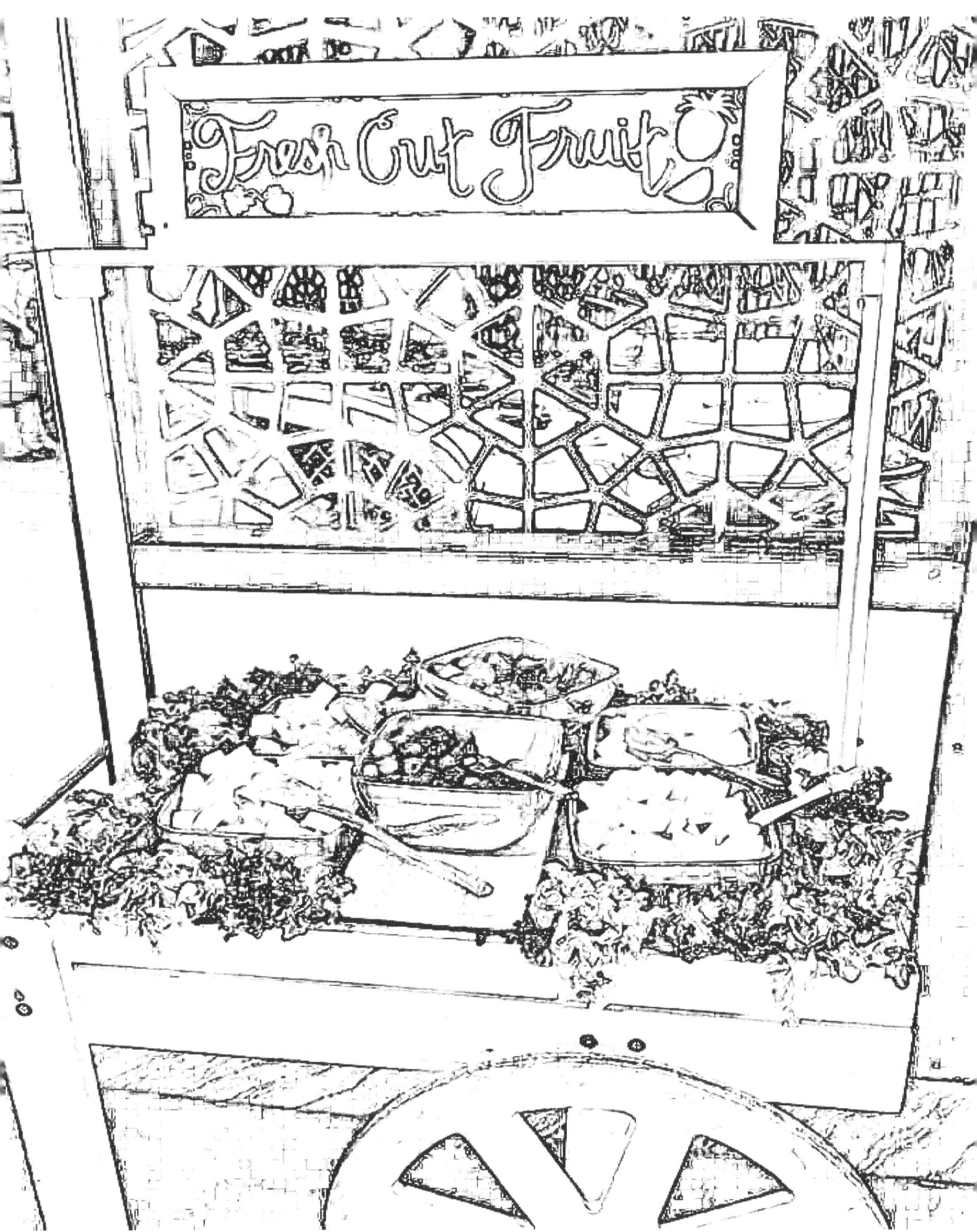

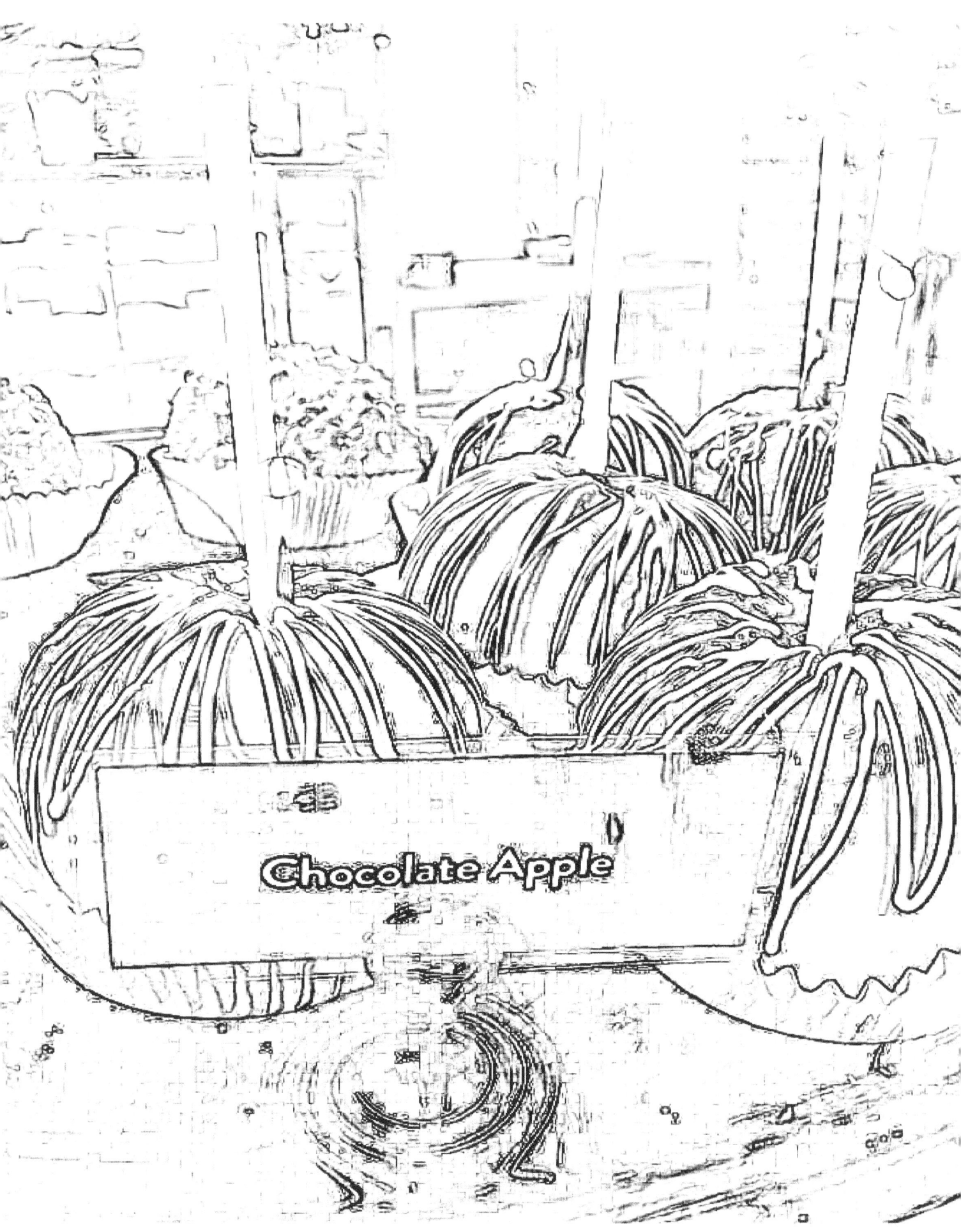

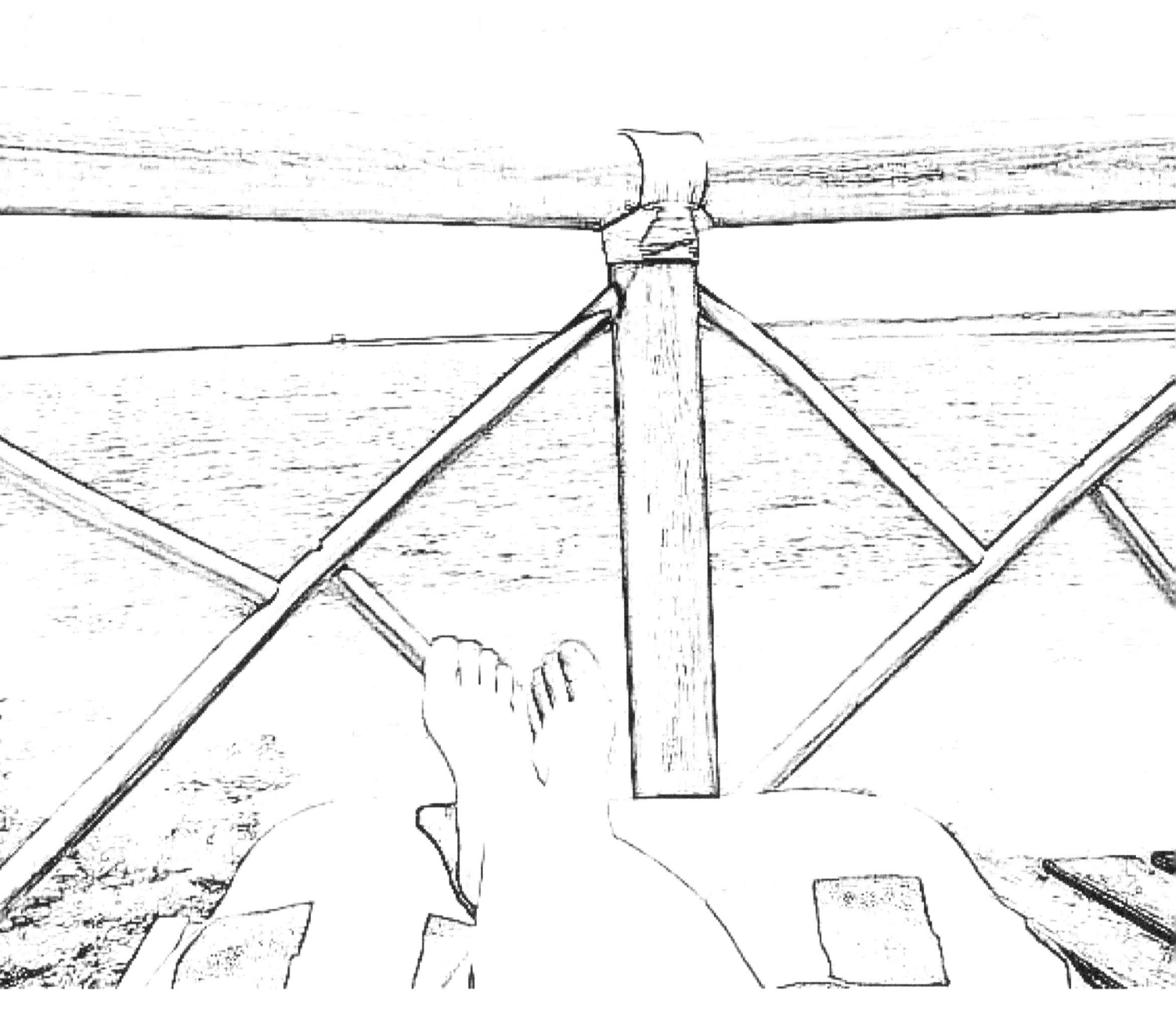

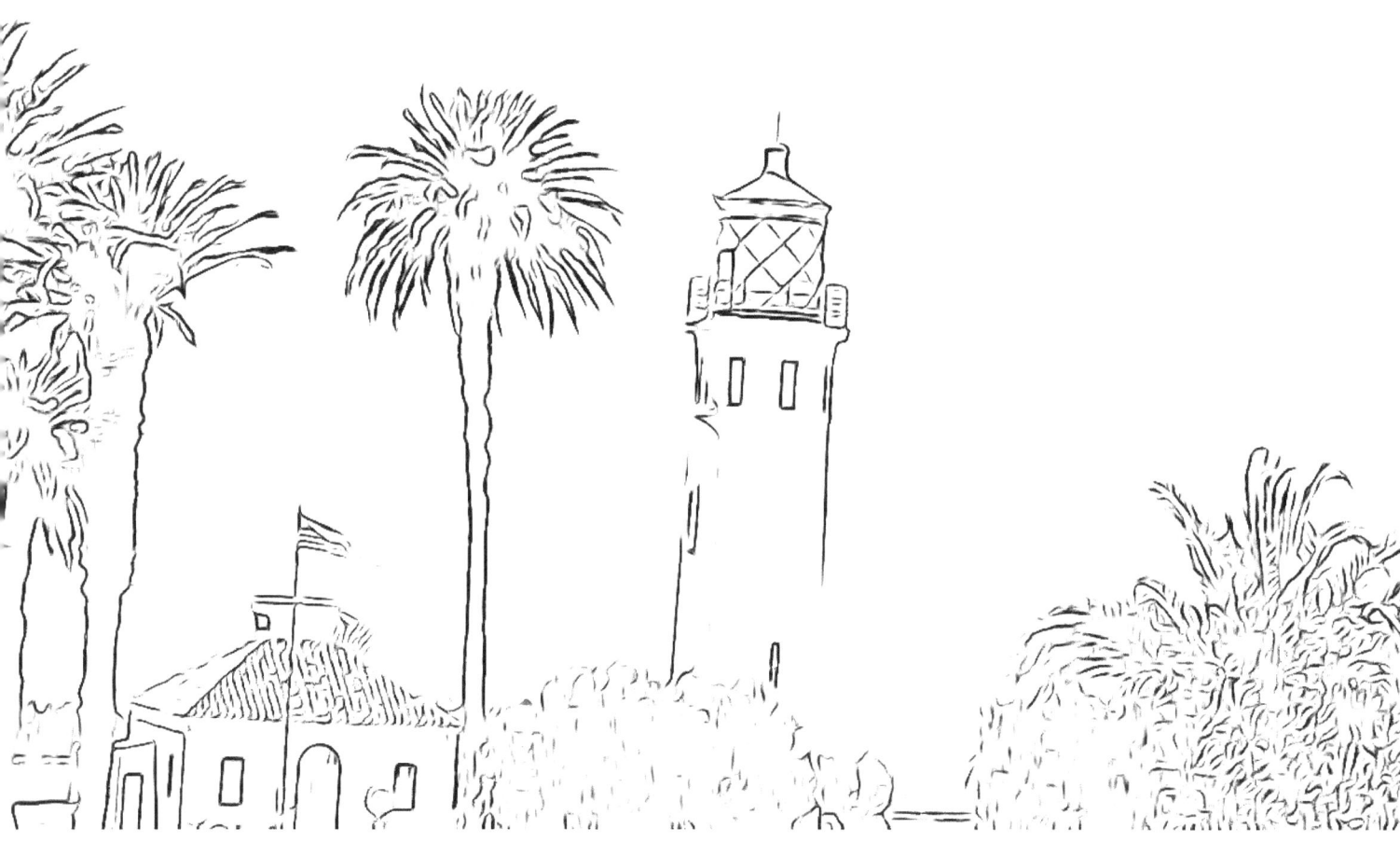

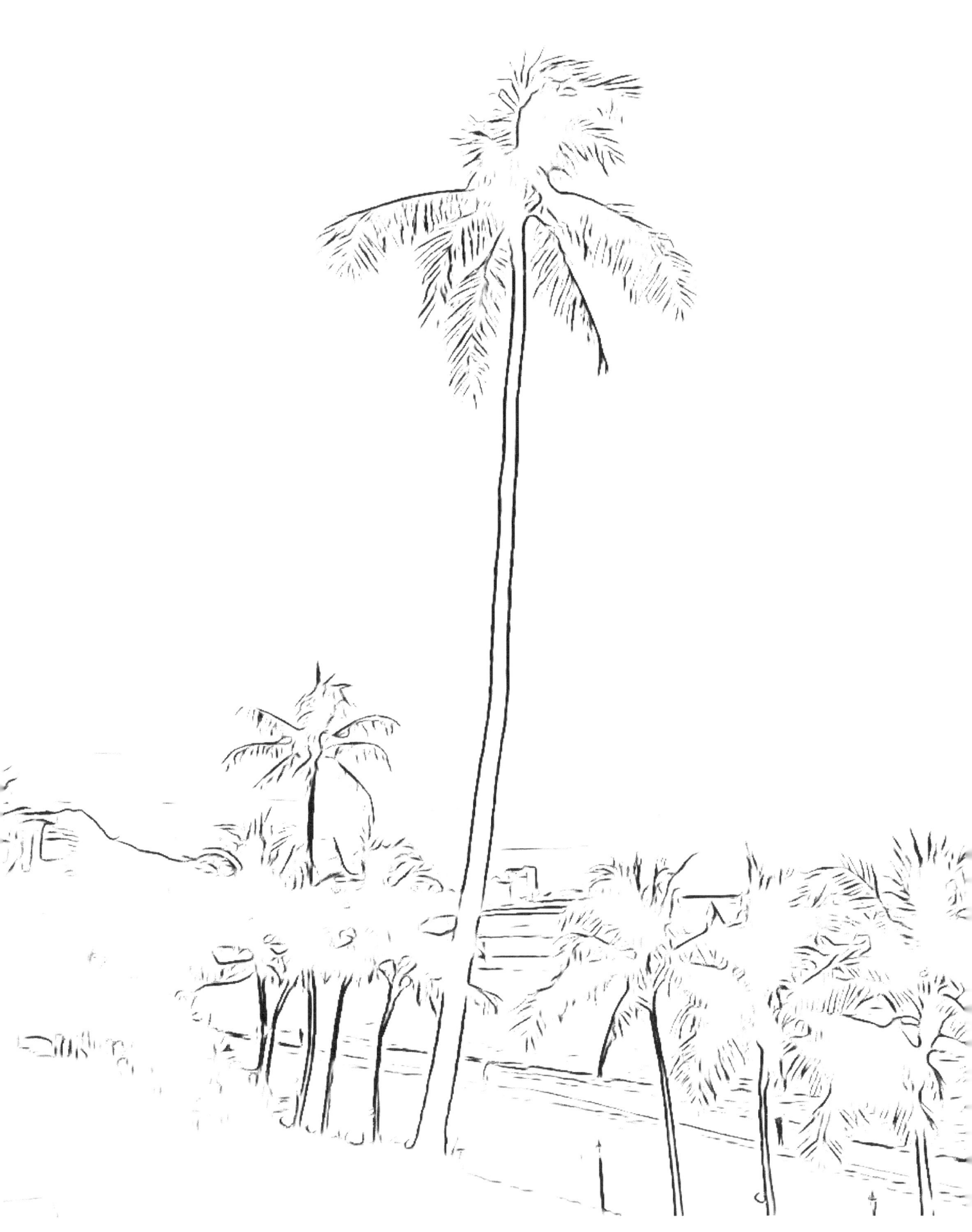

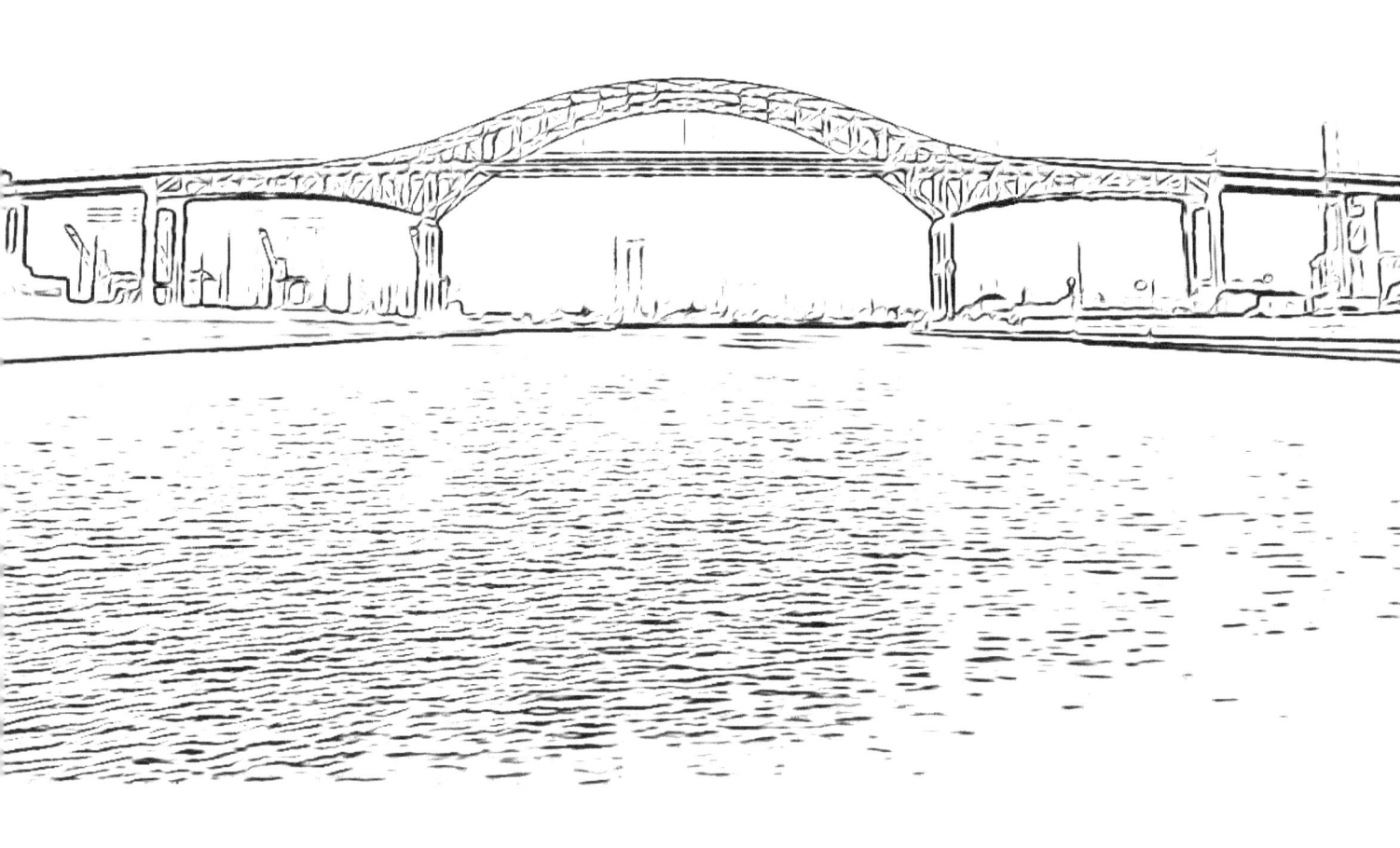

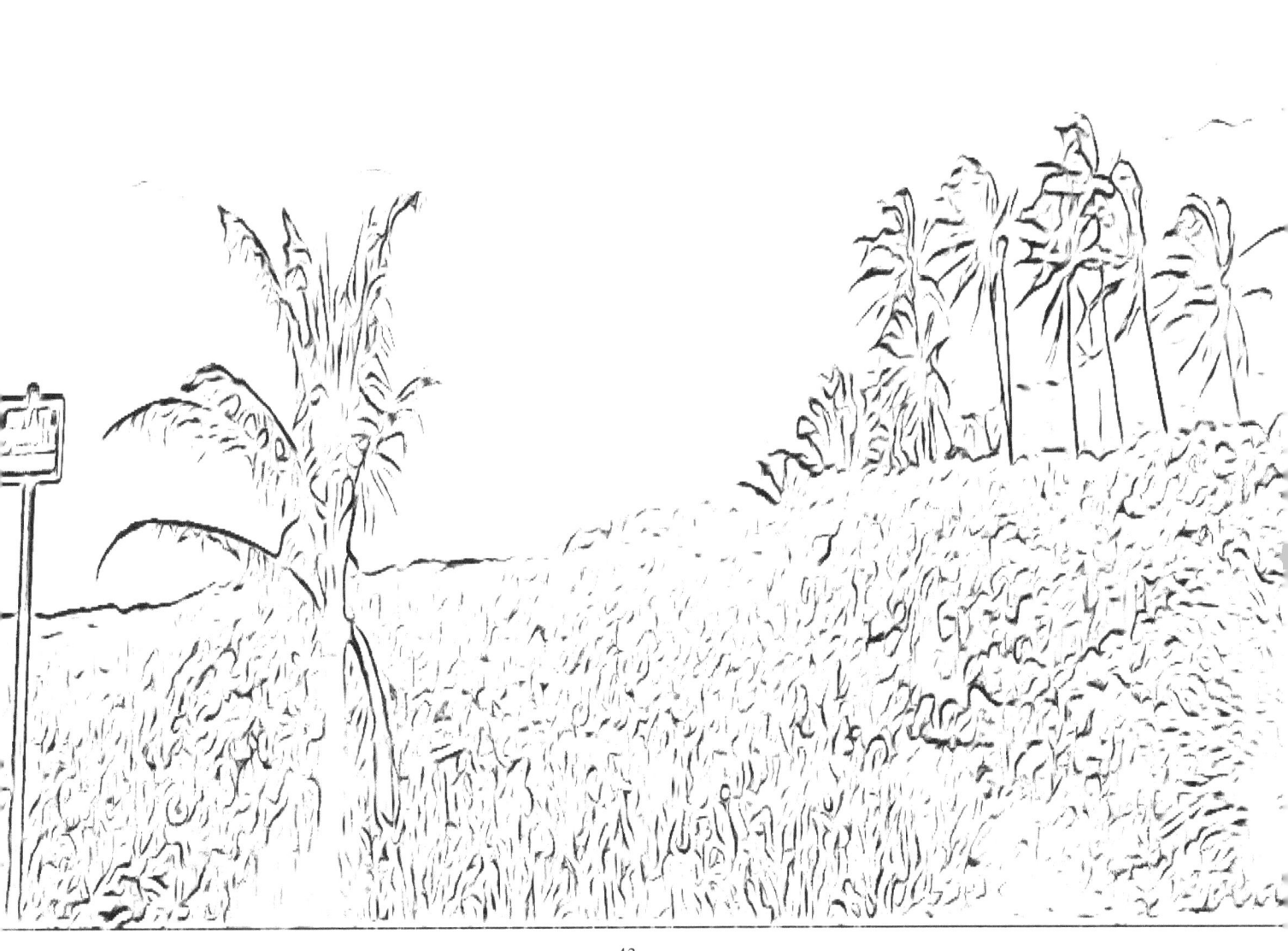

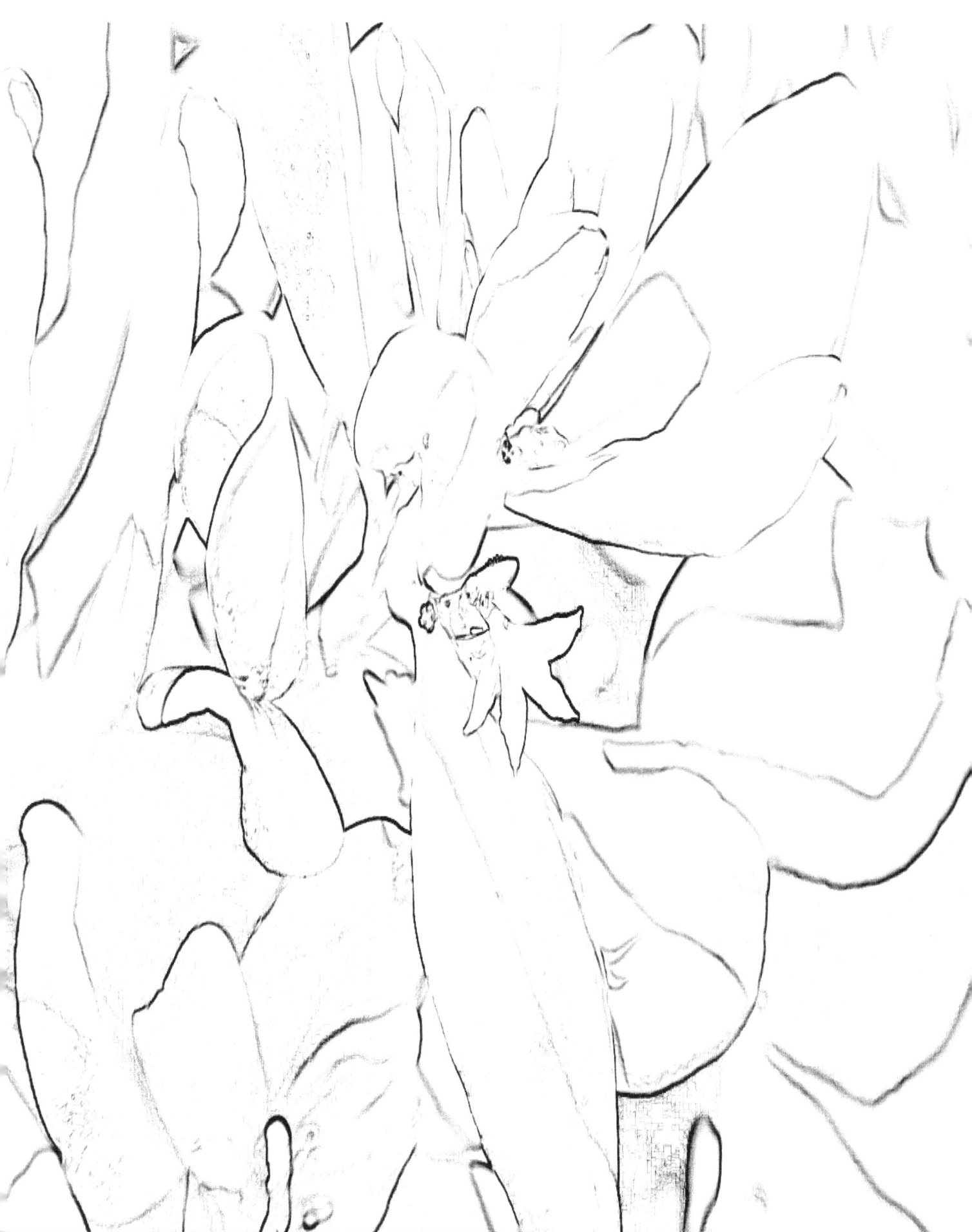

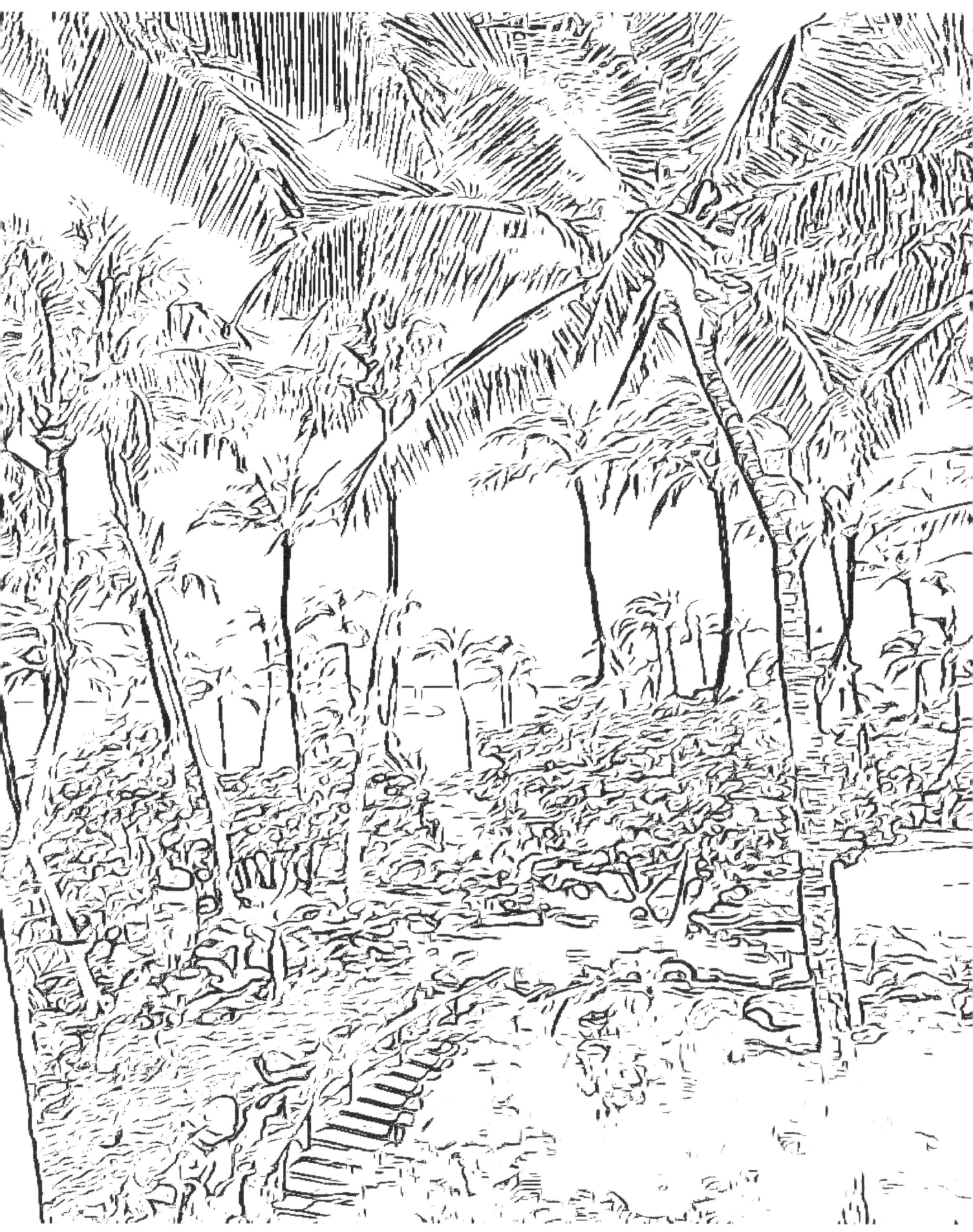

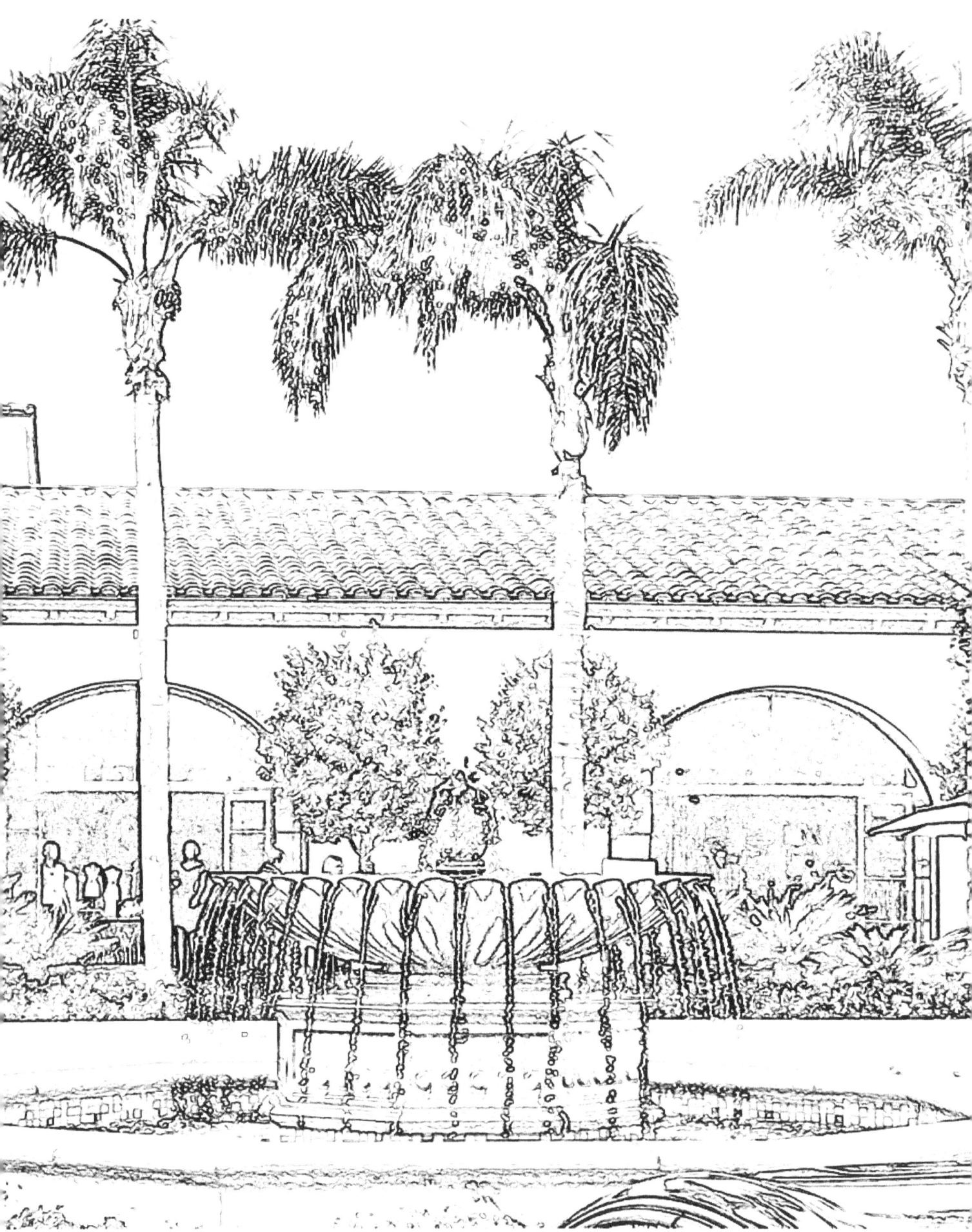

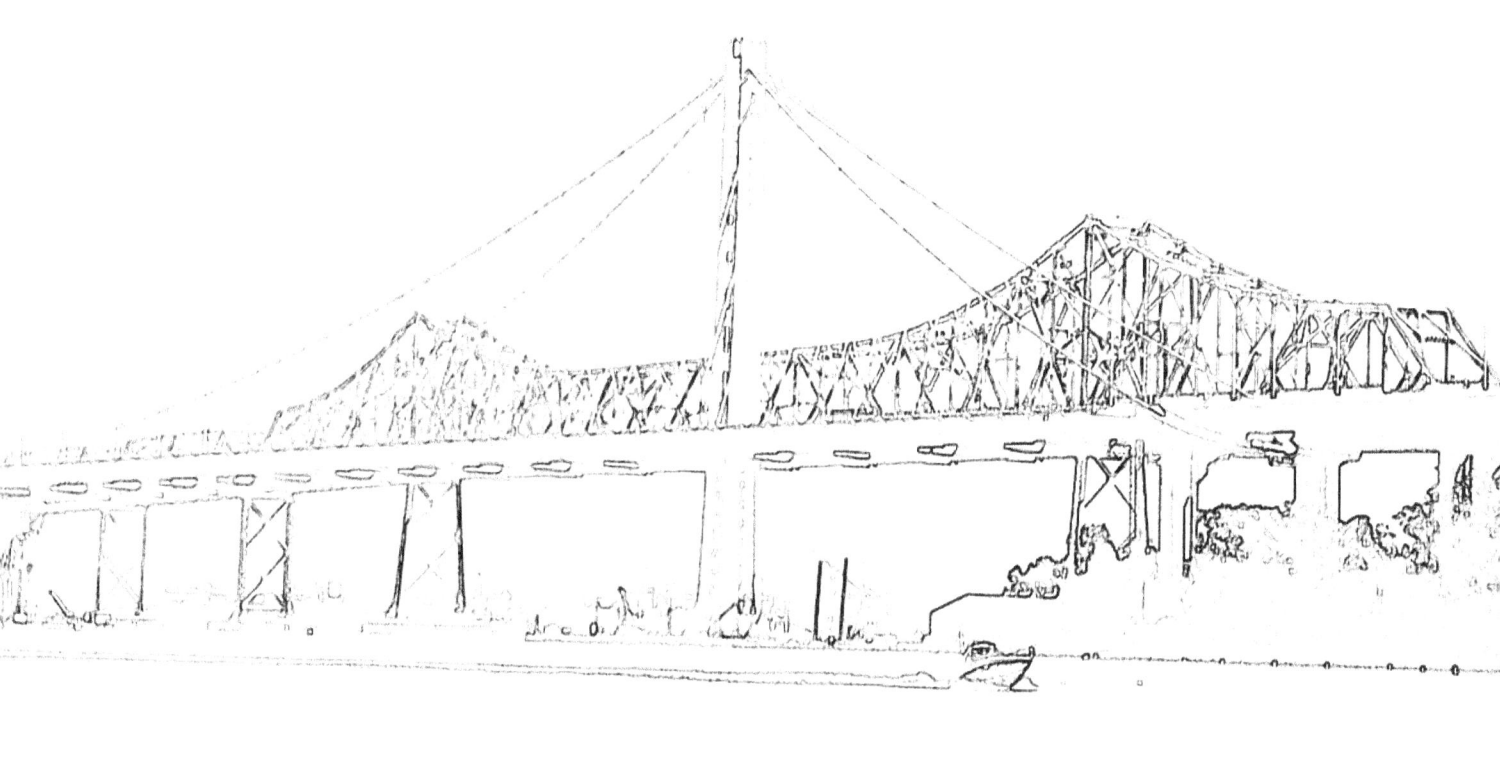

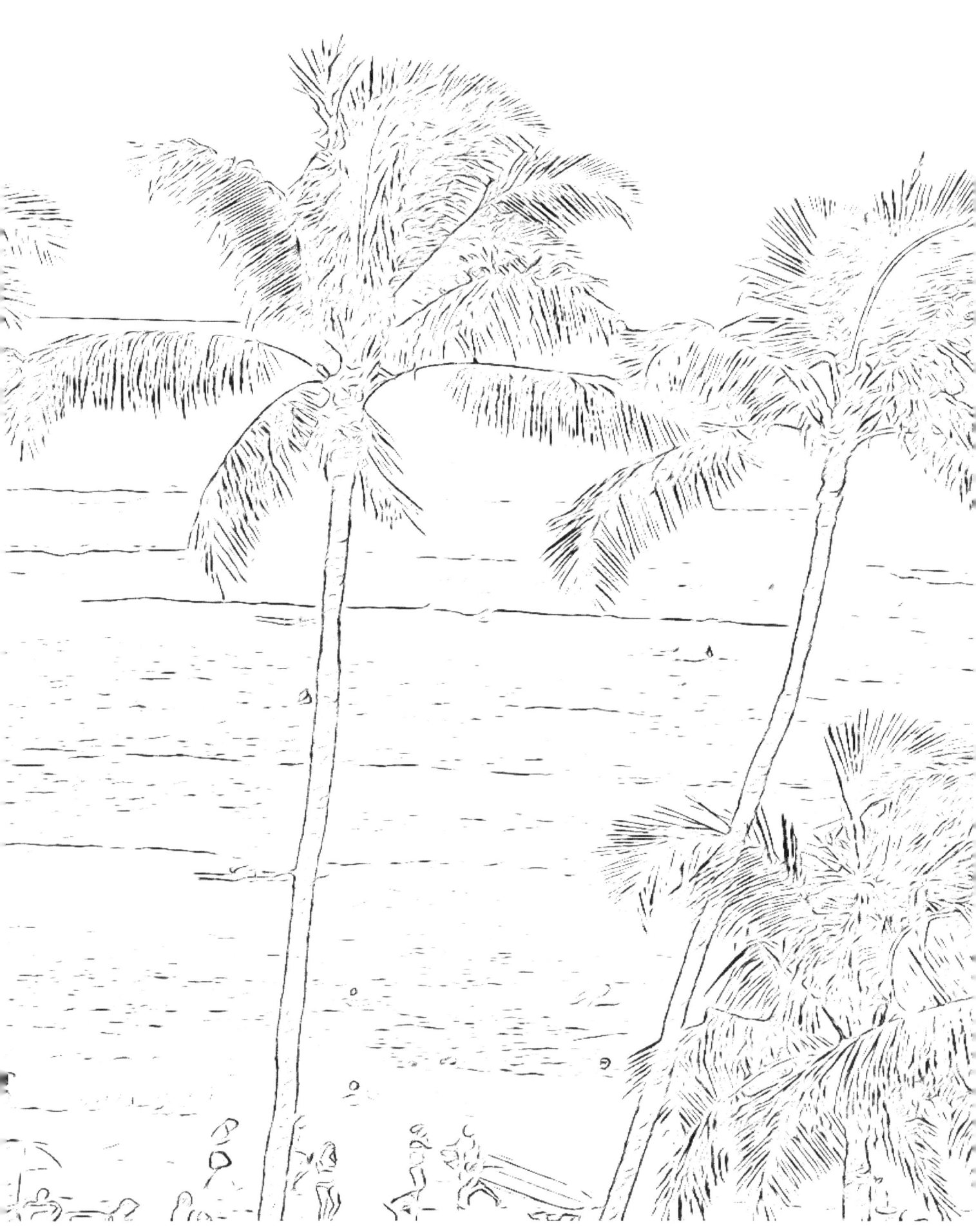

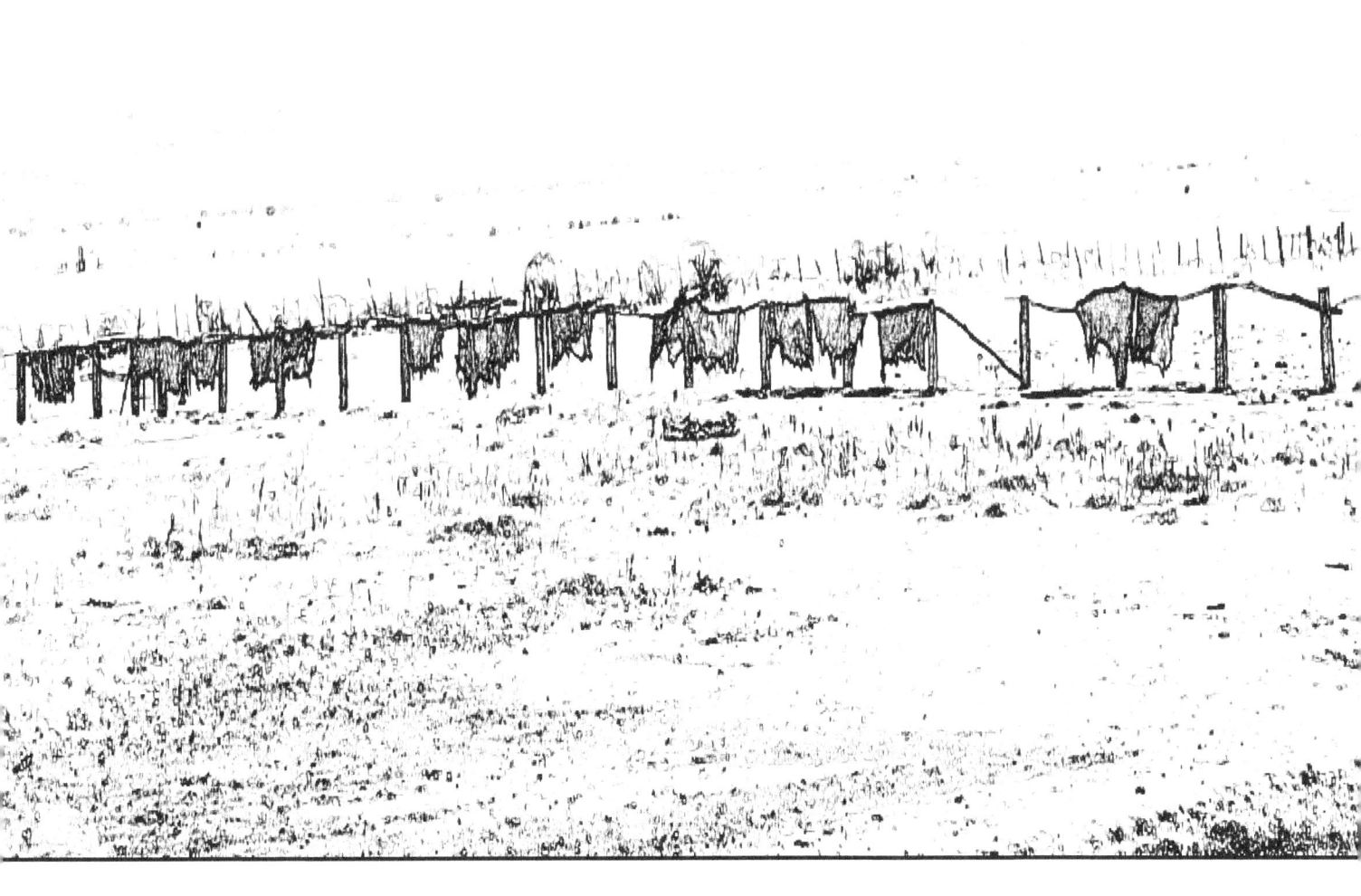

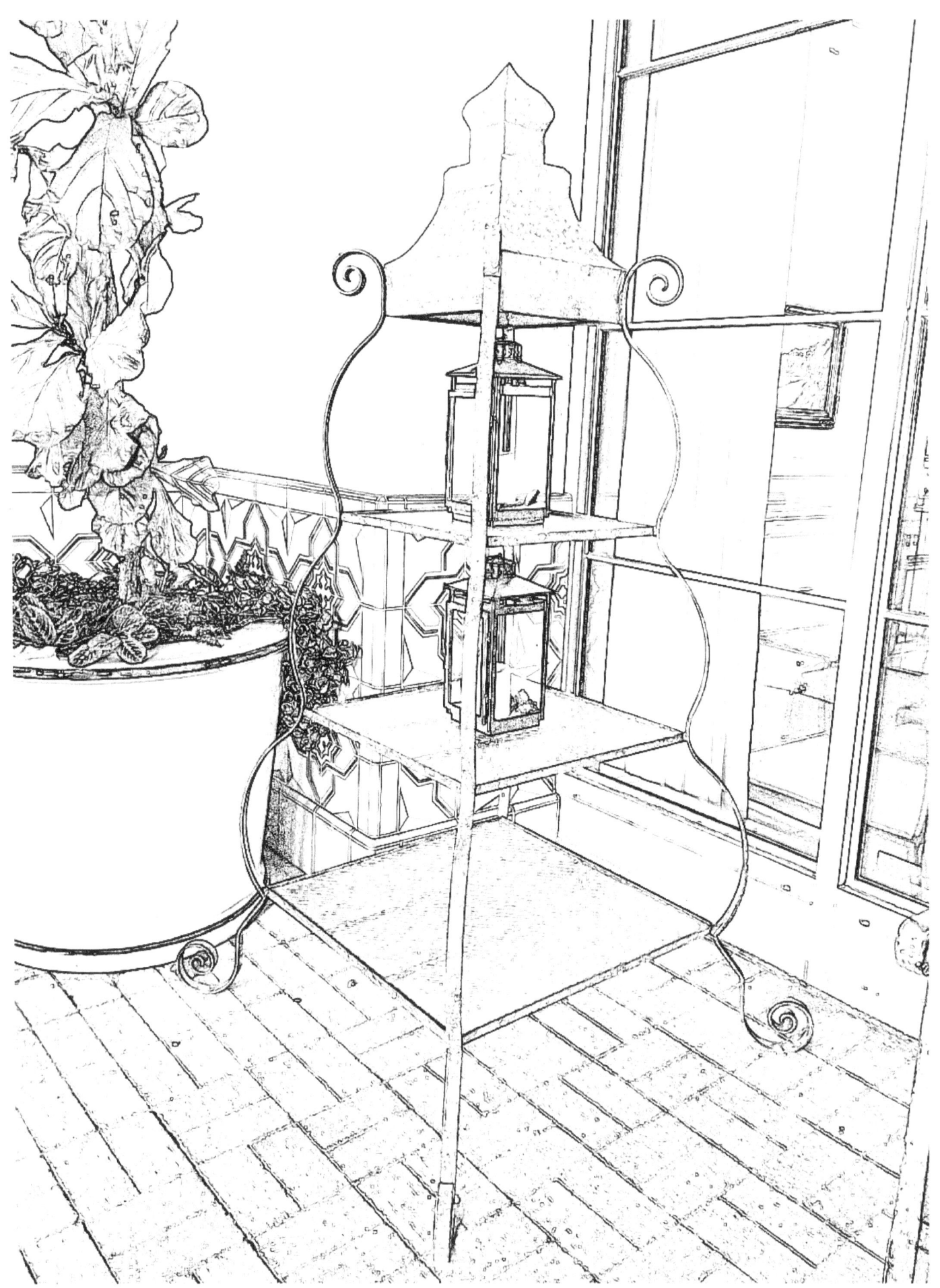

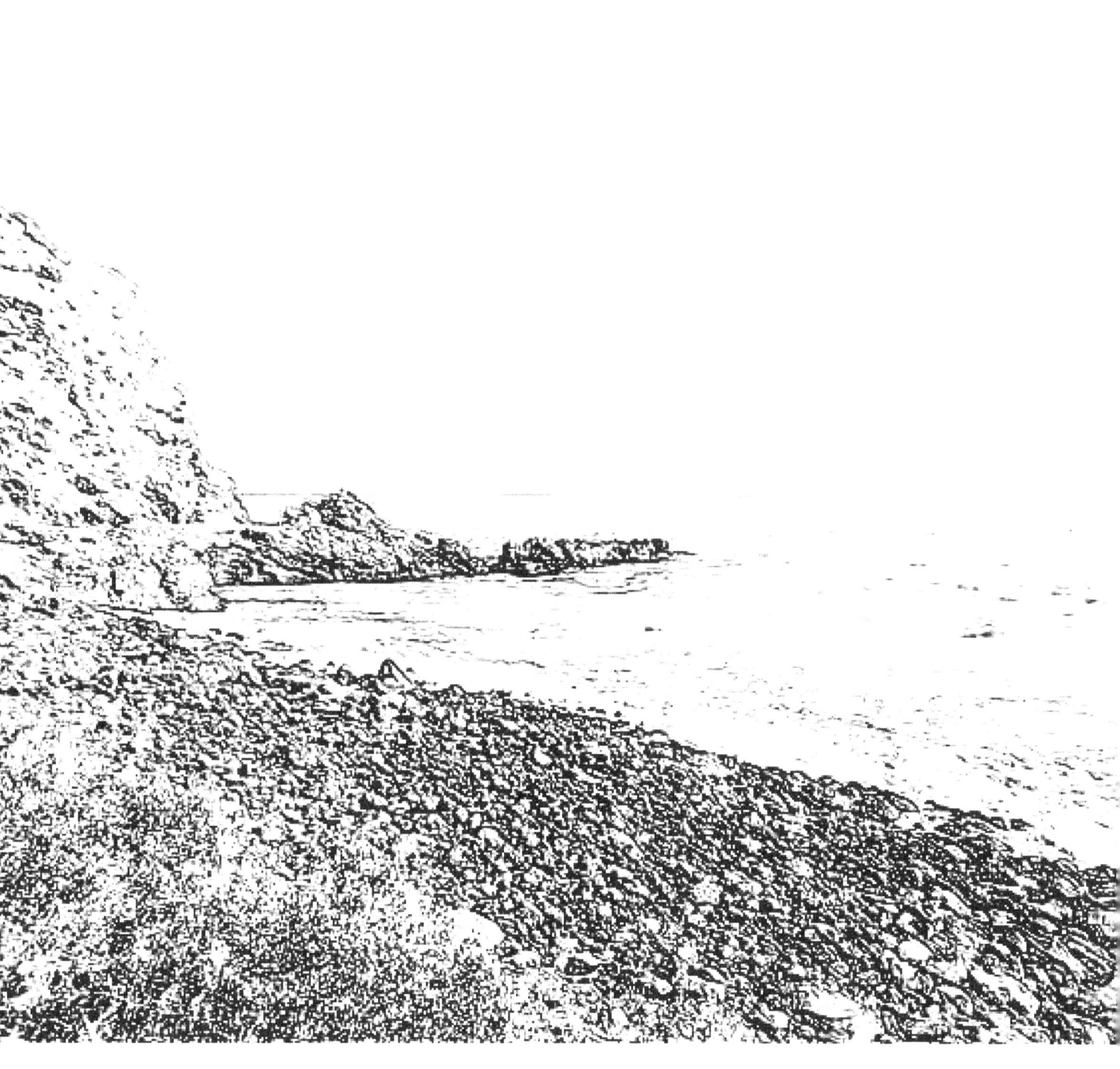

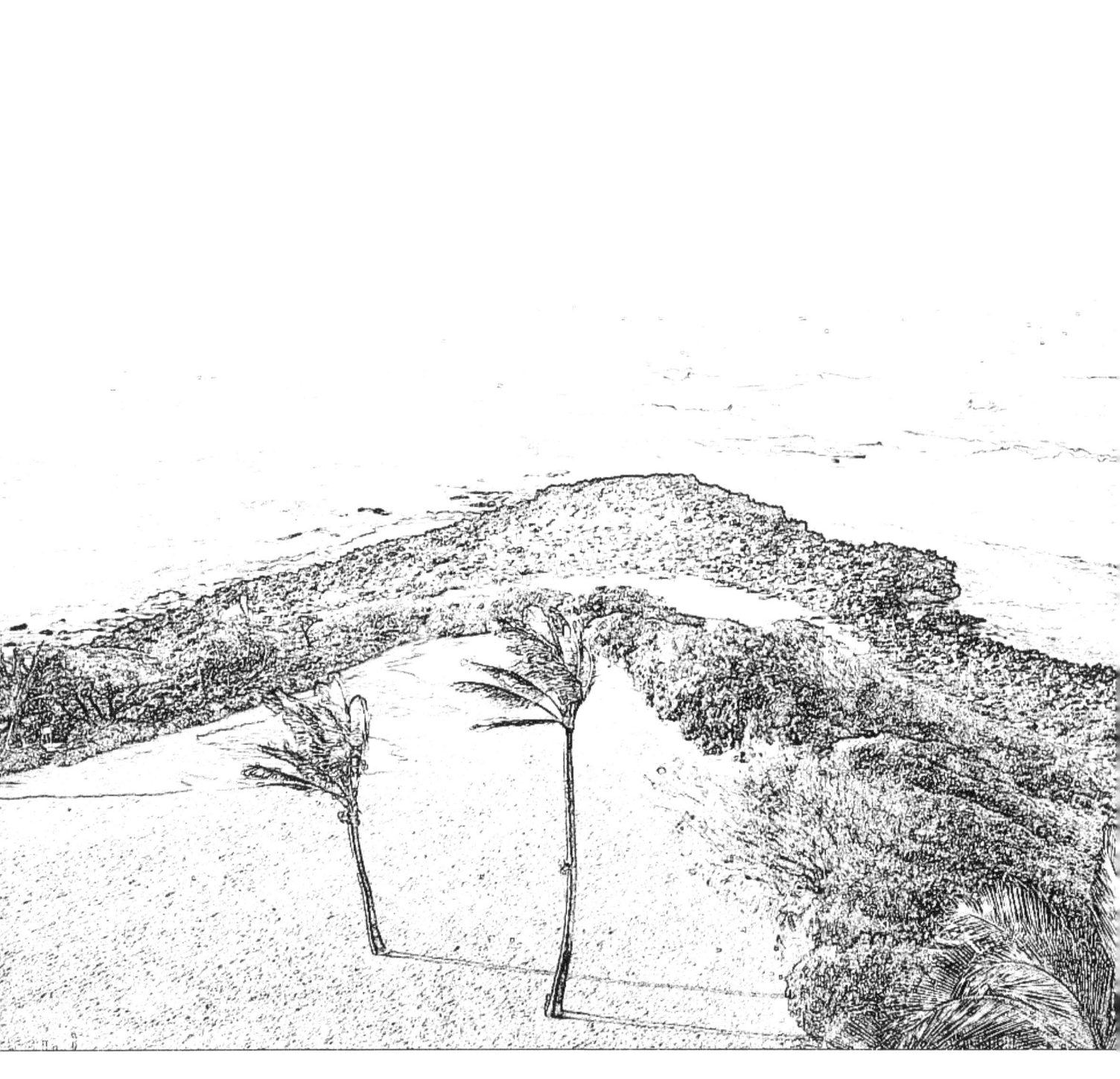

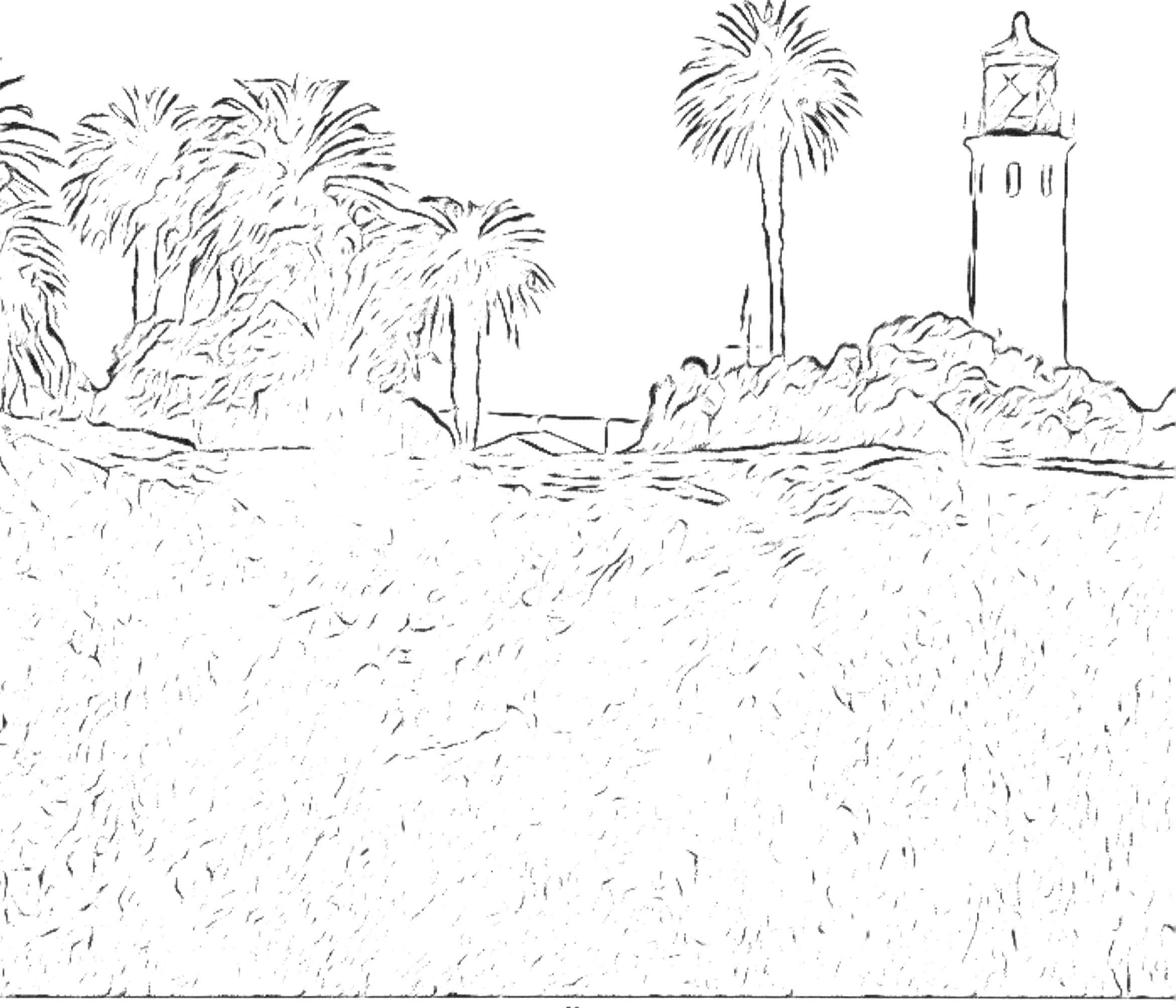

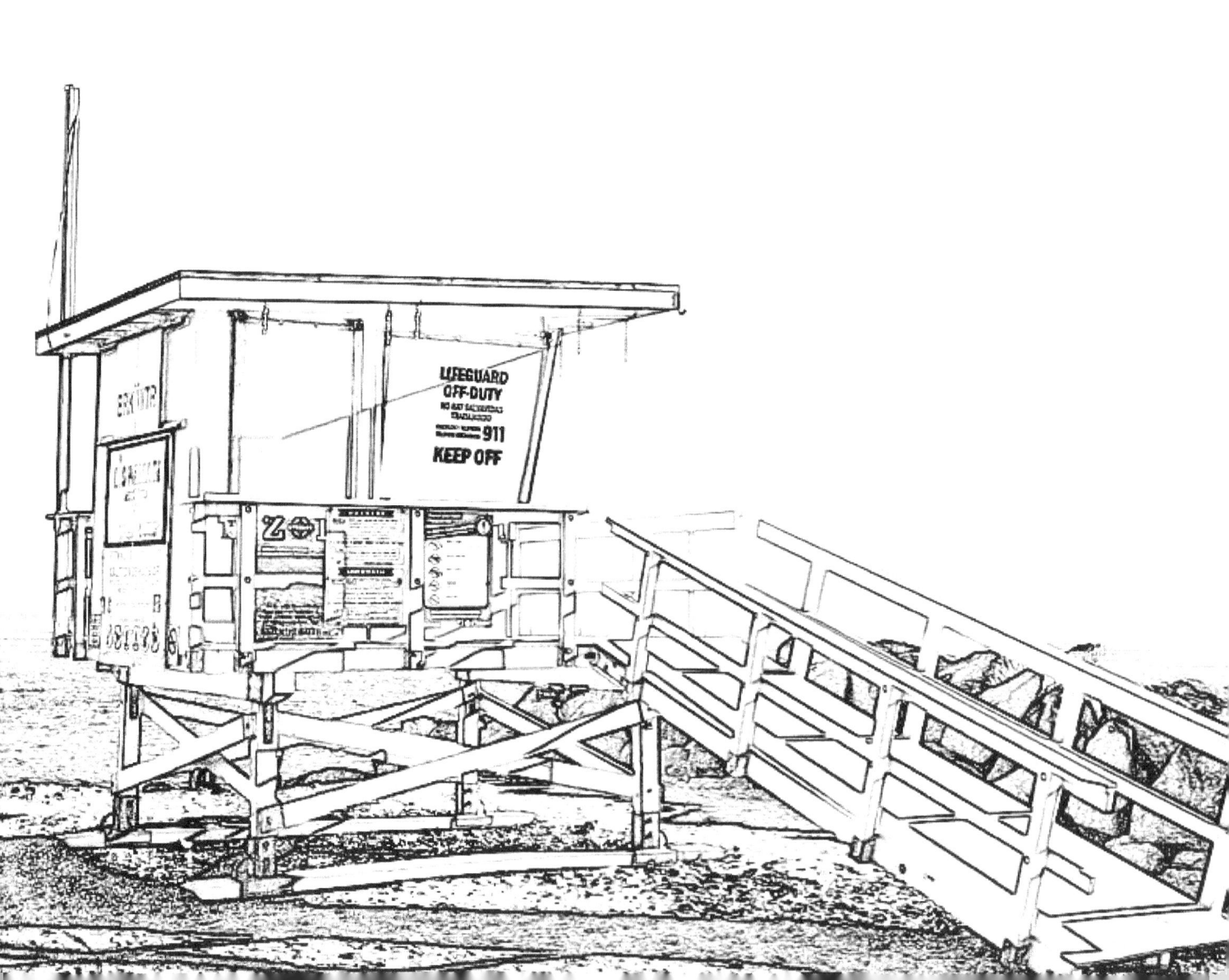

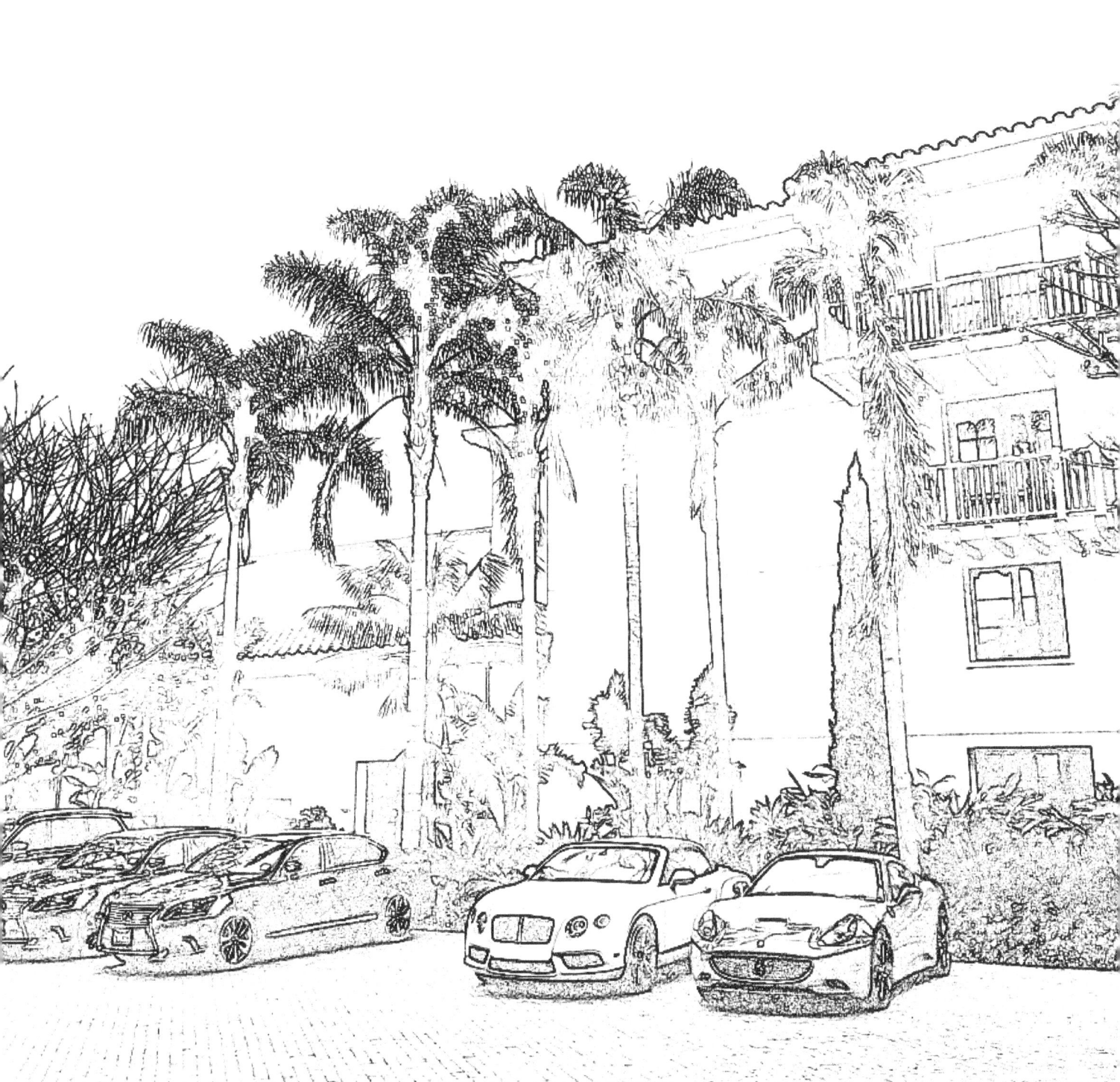

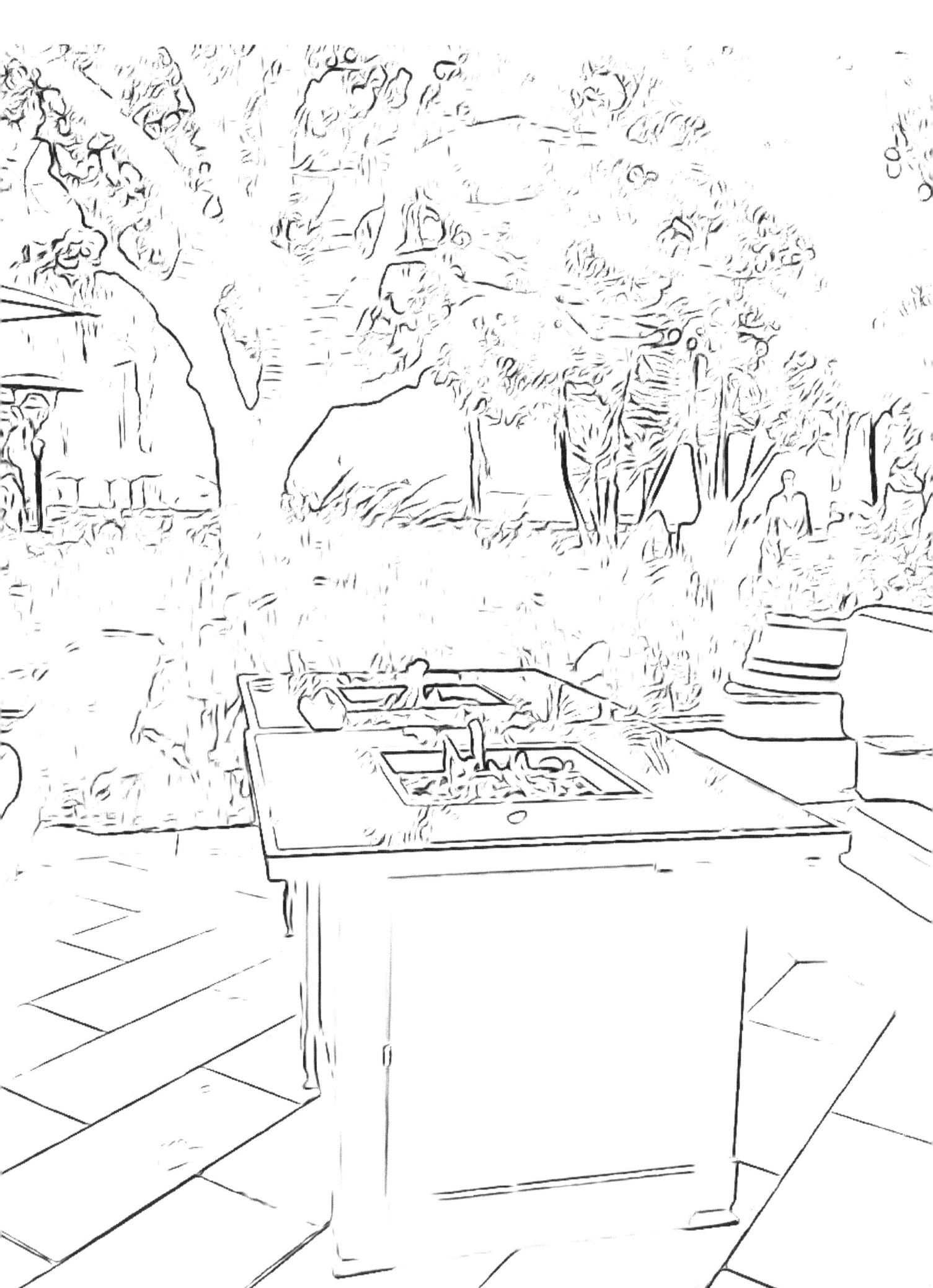

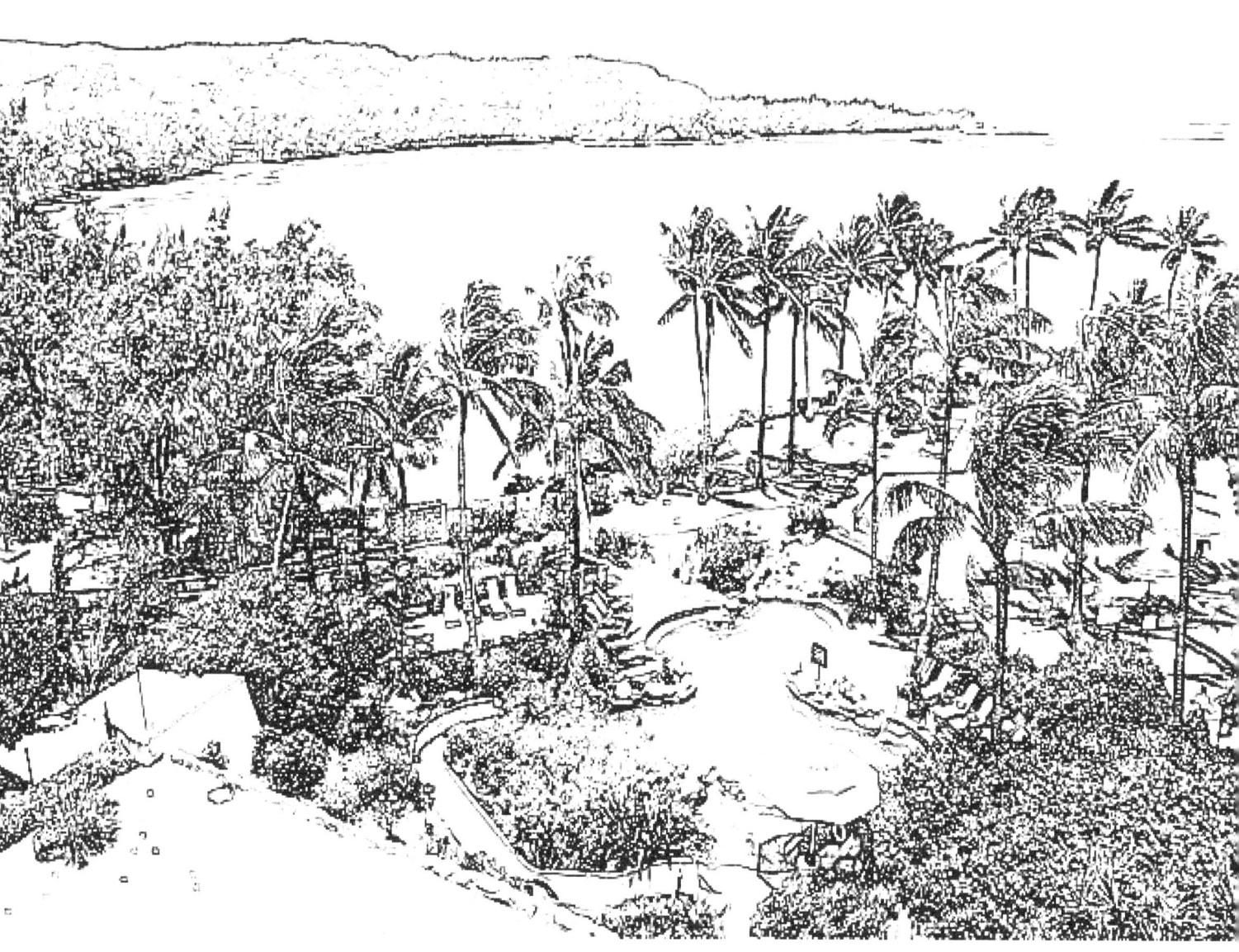

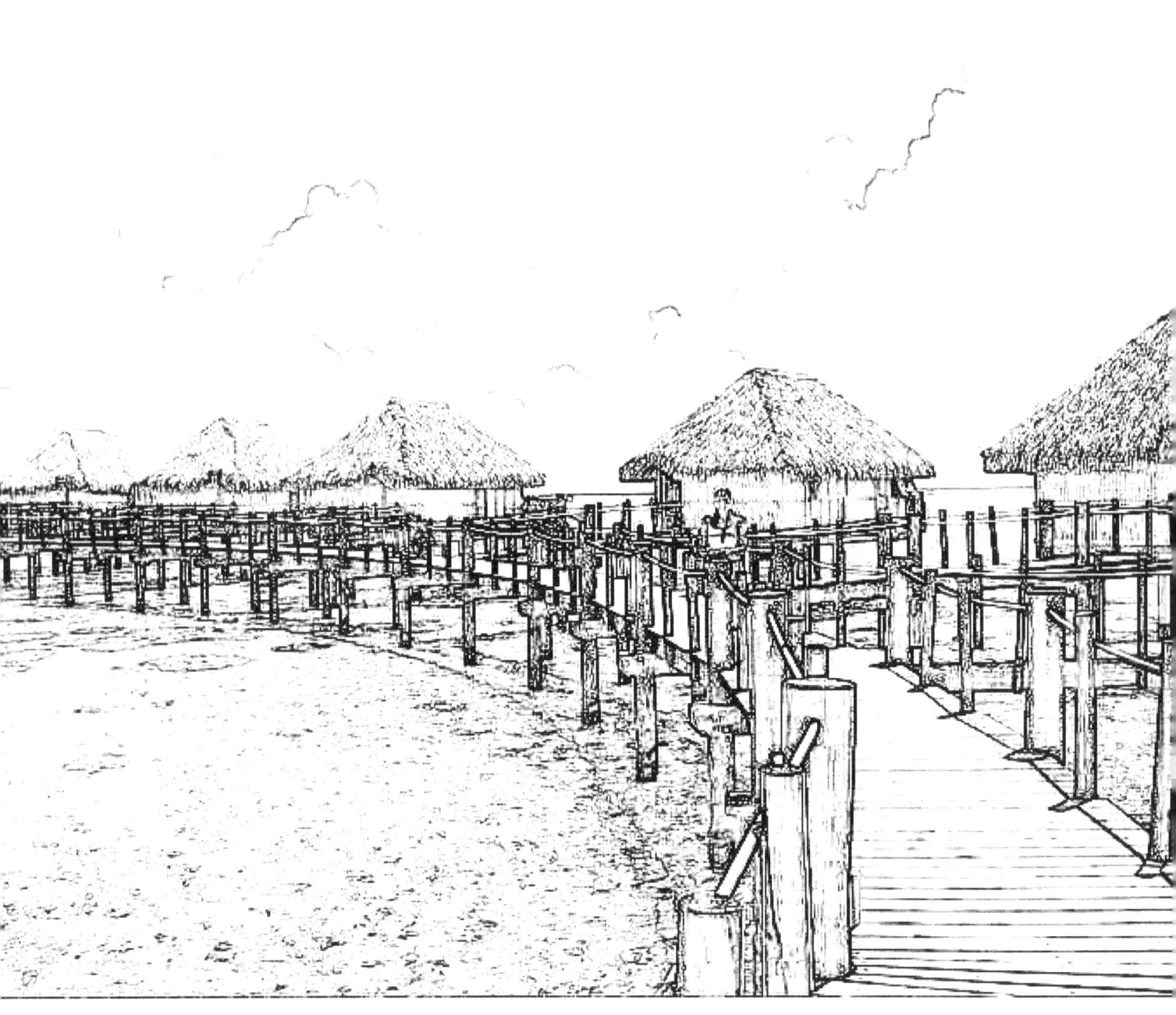

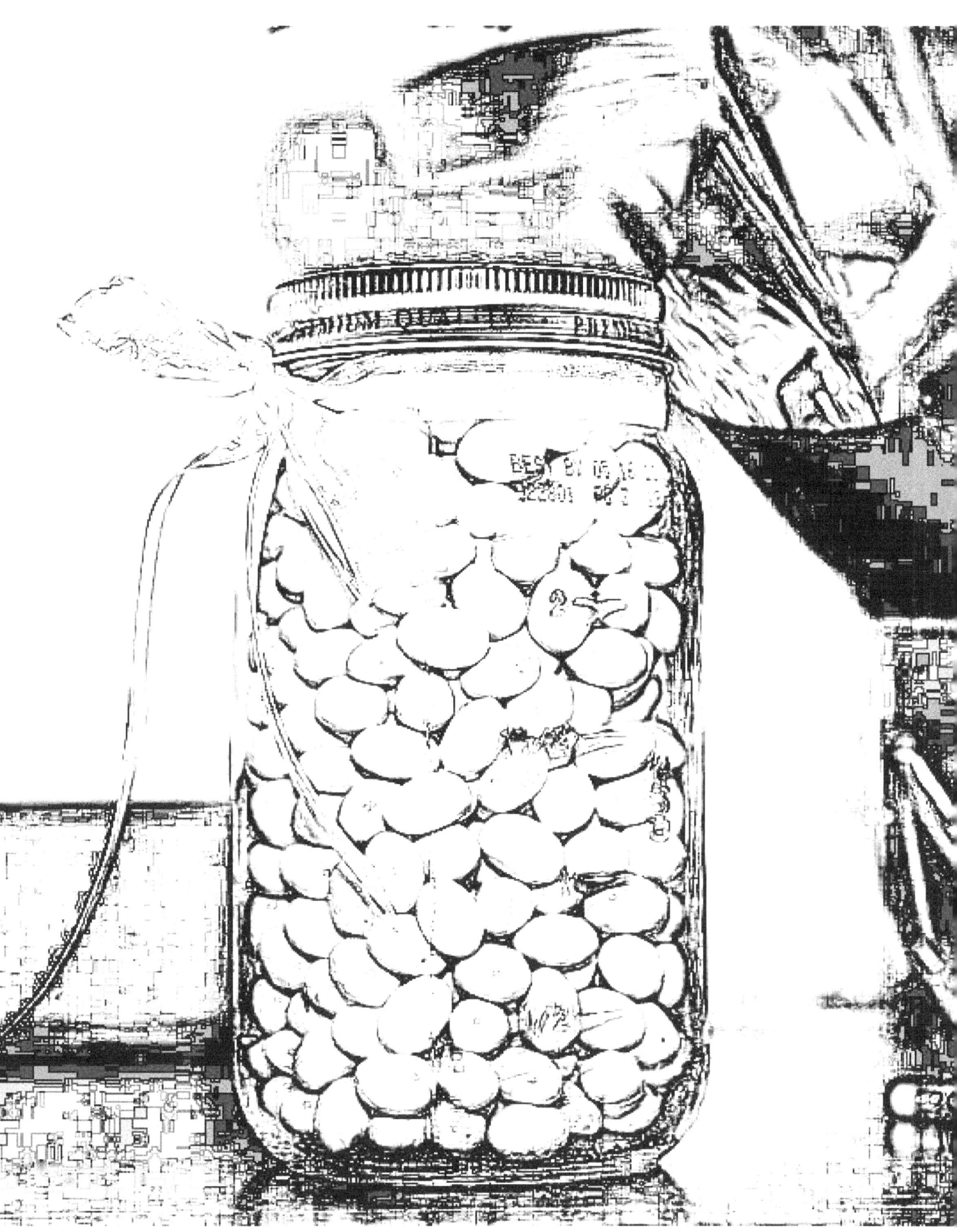

ABOUT THE AUTHORS

Sally Canario and Summer Canario live in Southern California and travel frequently for vacation. Mother and daughter enjoy traveling with their family to tropical places. Recharging is important to help relax and level set. The next best thing to vacation is to remember those happy times and places.

www.ingramcontent.com/pod-product-compliance
Lightning Source LLC
Chambersburg PA
CBHW080546190526
45169CB00007B/2661